PRAISE FOR
THE SUCCESS BOOK

"A quadruple espresso comprehensive self-help training manual."
Robert Craven – Managing Director, www.DirectorsCentre.com

"Tim's book is clear concise and thought provoking, but it's far more than that... he provides real world examples and a practical guide on how to take stock of who you are, what makes you tick, what drives and motivates you. We are all so different, we don't live by other peoples' measures. A great read - a great guide to life and your own - authentic success."
Steve Clarke CEO – www.EurekaSelling.co.uk

"Tim Johnson has survived some harrowing experiences in his own life. From these he has developed techniques that can help all of us improve our lives both at home and at work. A clear, concise and insightful book that everyone would benefit from reading."
Dr Mark Helme – BA Oxon, MRCP, MRCGP

"I read a lot of self development books and I can say hands down that in this short format Tim has covered pretty much everything in a very accessible way. I found it insightful and full of great tips and information."
Sara Taheri – Editorial Director www.LIDpublishing.com

"Tim's insights on personal mastery, coming from his personal journey, are incisive. If you want to organise what goes on inside your head to make you more successful and happy then The Success Book is a must read."
Martin Davies – Co-Founder, www.nrg-networks.com

"Tim explores the numerous and complex elements that affect the pursuit of and contribute to the achievement of success. Through sharing his own insights, based on his own experiences (both in life and in business) through referencing many valuable models, quotes and publications (some well known and some not) and through posing pointed and thought provoking questions, Tim takes us on a journey of deep self reflection and self insight and suggests strategies and tactics to enable us to navigate both the triumphs and disasters en route to genuine success."

Tamsen Garrie – Managing Director, www.Alpha-Associates.biz

"Many talk about success, but true success covers ALL parts of your life, not just money. Tim has captured all the different areas perfectly to help us understand what success truly is. However, we all know success does come at a price & dealing with disasters in our life is part of that. Rarely is this addressed in such a productive way, Tim has done that in this book. Great read!"

Baiju Solanki – CEO & Founder EnSpirit Inc. www.baijusolanki.com

"It's Terrific!"

My mum – (Julia Aston-Smith)

"We see thousands of people starting businesses every single year yet the majority fail within the first 3 years. Tim has created a blue print for success here that gives everyone a fighting chance to make a real go of it. Using his template you will create better balance in your life, abundance and deeper relationships both in your business and personal lives.Tim demonstrates his wealth of experience and shares practical, easy to implement ideas relevant to all. A must read for all those serious about achieving success."

Warren Cass – Founder of www.Business-Scene.com and www.ChampionsOfSmallBusiness.co.uk

HOW TO
USE THIS BOOK

This book is deceptively condensed, with each short chapter
worthy of a day or more's careful reflection.

There are a number of different ways of using the book.
Some people read the whole book and then return to do the
exercises they feel are most relevant... some people start at
exercise one and work their way through every one. If your issue is
loss of mojo, then the best exercises are 12, 17, and 32.
If you are at a crisis in your relationships, then the best exercises
are... 6, 9 and 19 and if you want to get clear on your
goals go to chapters 15, 16 and 33.

Above all, enjoy, think for yourself, dip in dip out, and
return regularly. After all this is a lifetime's work.

THANKS

I've been privileged to meet so many people on my journey through work, workshops, networking and sport along with extended friends and family – each one of you has made an impact on me in one way or another, thank you.

Particular mentions go to Frank Taylor for believing in me and being instrumental in my recovery from the accident. My close team at 4Networking: Tamsen Garrie, Chas Jordan, Daryl & Paula Hine, Gary Johannes and Ali Hollands who have all gone on to do great things. Mimi Avery for when I arrived in Bristol, Ruth Steggles founder of Fresh Air Fridays for her unrelenting support, Charles Maddren for reaching out when it most mattered. Dave Stone and Jacqui Stearn for bringing impartial views mid book writing. Nikki, Sara and Charlotte from the LID team who massively helped to get me here and to get over the finishing line. The Bristol Town and County Harriers for their help and inspiration, and for introducing me to the marvels of off-road running. And finally to Julie Freke for believing in me as I venture out on the next leg of my journey.

**TO
JACK, KATE AND JESSICA**

THE SUCCESS BOOK

HOW TO GROW YOURSELF AND YOUR BUSINESS

TIM JOHNSON

LONDON
MADRID
MEXICO CITY

NEW YORK
BARCELONA
MONTERREY
SHANGHAI

BOGOTA
BUENOS AIRES
SAN FRANCISCO

Published by
LID Publishing Ltd
One Adam Street
London
WC2N 6LE
United Kingdom

31 West 34th Street, Suite 8004,
New York, NY 1001, US

info@lidpublishing.com
www.lidpublishing.com

A member of:

BPR

Business Publishers Roundtable

www.businesspublishersroundtable.com

Printed in the Czech Republic by Finidr

ISBN: 978-1-907794-98-8

Cover and page design: Laura Hawkins

CONTENTS

PREFACE

The first thing I can remember is standing at the side of the road looking down at my upended Lexus 400, wondering what to do next. I was clutching my arm, which was flapping from the shoulder and the elbow, while shock eliminated the pain. The following day, the surgeon apologized for amputating my right arm at the elbow. I felt lucky, I was alive, I was left-handed and I had expected to lose my whole arm.

But my luck turned: MRSA, a litigation battle over the value of my shares in the £4 million business I'd helped grow from a start-up, and opiate addiction from the pain relief.

Physical recovery, healing the broken arm at the shoulder, took two years. I went from taking five minutes to climb a flight of stairs to completing an Olympic-distance triathlon. Mental recovery involved an MBA and mediation training, emotional recovery, counselling and the start of a long personal development journey.

Business recovery allowed me to work in the areas of tax, insolvency, franchising and turnaround work, and in 2006, I co-founded the business breakfast network, 4Networking. I set the foundations, business model, strategy and systems to allow it to grow from an idea to a complete national network in a few short years, with a turnover in excess of £3 million.

After selling my stake in 4networking, and drawing my 26-year relationship with my wife to a natural conclusion, I took time out to research, reflect and recover from a full-on journey of success, setbacks, and resilience. This book explores how self-leadership, strategic leadership and leading others all combine in the journey of success.

INTRODUCTION: WHAT IS SUCCESS?

According to Wikipedia, success is a term denoting the achievement of aims or attainment of goals, or levels of social status, and is often used specifically to mean financial profitability. People who achieve their goals are frequently termed "successes".

What does success mean to you? In simple terms, you could say it's knowing what you want and getting it, but if it were that simple there'd be no need to write this book. To use the 'law of attraction', people tell us all we have to do is "ask, believe and receive", but I've yet to see the mass of people getting results that way.

It is easy to get caught in the hamster-wheel existence of working harder to gain more status and money, to buy more stuff; only to find that, at the end of the day, most of the stuff means stuff all, and meanwhile you've lost sight of what life's all about and are exhausted.

"THE PLAIN FACT IS THAT THE PLANET DOES NOT NEED MORE SUCCESSFUL PEOPLE. BUT IT DOES DESPERATELY NEED MORE PEACEMAKERS, HEALERS, RESTORERS, STORYTELLERS, AND LOVERS OF EVERY KIND. IT NEEDS PEOPLE WHO LIVE WELL IN THEIR PLACES. IT NEEDS PEOPLE OF MORAL COURAGE WILLING TO JOIN THE FIGHT TO MAKE THE WORLD HABITABLE AND

HUMANE. AND THESE QUALITIES HAVE LITTLE TO DO WITH
SUCCESS AS OUR CULTURE HAS DEFINED IT."
David W. Orr, author of *Earth in Mind: On Education, Environment,*
and *The Human Prospect*

"IF YOU CAN MEET WITH TRIUMPH AND DISASTER
AND TREAT THOSE TWO IMPOSTERS JUST THE SAME...
YOURS IS THE EARTH AND EVERYTHING THAT'S IN IT"
(extract from **Rudyard Kipling**'s poem, *IF*)

So there are two sides to success: creating triumphs and dealing with disasters. They are different skill sets. But success is an individual thing, so before you know what you want, you need to know who you are.

This book is divided into four sections:

1. PERSONAL MASTERY

Getting to know and understand yourself better so you become more in tune with your core essence and less blown about by other people and events. This will help you identify the right path for you more clearly.

2. CREATING TRIUMPHS

Clarifying what you want, and the ways of being and doing that help achieve this.

3. DEALING WITH DISASTER

The journey is never plain sailing all the way; dealing with setbacks is part of the path to success. In fact, the more able you are to deal with setbacks, the more able you are to embrace life whole-heartedly and make things happen.

4. SPECIFIC SKILLS FROM THE CONCISE ADVICE SERIES

The LID publishing stable has a wealth of specific advice that can help you progress towards your personal success. This chapter provides a synopsis of the other books in the series on which to feast.

For me, success is about getting to know who I am on a deeper level, growing to love and accept myself as I am, learning not to pass responsibility for my happiness to other people. From that place, I can embark on a journey that leads me to become a more expansive version of myself, and helps me to live a richer and broader life.

Does this resonate with you? Then let's begin...

CHAPTER ONE

PERSONAL
MASTERY

1. PERSONAL MASTERY

"I AM THE MASTER OF MY FATE, I AM THE CAPTAIN OF MY SOUL"
(William Ernest Henley)

This means that to master your fate, you need to be the captain of your soul, and you need to know how to run your own ship – a lifetime's work!

Ultimately, if success is knowing what you want and setting out to achieve it, it makes sense to get to know yourself better so you'll have more chance of recognizing the things YOU want, rather than what your partners, peers or parents want, or what society conditions you to want. Next, you must develop some self-leadership skills to navigate the journey and be less blown about by people, events and circumstances along the way.

In this section we touch upon:

AUTHENTICITY: Who am I? This enquiry can be viewed from many perspectives, and doing so naturally yields new insights

ATTITUDE: Your attitude, not your aptitude, will determine your altitude

AWARENESS: The better able you are to sense what is going on, both internally and externally, the better decisions you'll be able to make

ACCEPTANCE: Much suffering is caused by our own resistance to what is; learning to understand acceptance on a deeper level allows you to proceed with more grace and less effort

APPRECIATION: What you appreciate, appreciates. Nurturing this skill is a foundation stone to a successful life

ATTACHMENT: Nothing in life is permanent and letting go of attachment to things we hold dear is a step towards liberation

ALIGNMENT: Aligning your head, heart and soul so you are truly comfortable in your own skin allows you to engage with others in balance and ensures you don't burn out

2. AUTHENTICITY

Authentic means being genuine or real. Who is the real you, the genuine article? What was the core essence of you before your upbringing, education and work added their imprints?

How do you know you are being authentic? When you are being your true self, of course. But who is your true self? In fact, who are you anyway? Are you your body? Are you your mind? Are you your collection of experiences to date? Are you the roles you play in life? Are you the stories you hold about yourself inside your head? Or are you the stories other people hold about you in their heads? What do you think?

Many of us lead our lives as if we are our identity. Our identities come in all shapes and sizes but there is a strong pull for many of us to be drawn into identities of high social standing, high incomes and a sizeable collection of tangible items and experiences to prove our significance. In other words, we are drawn to the conventional 'success identity', but what is your authentic self-identity?

We are who we choose to be. We have inherent gifts and talents with which we were born, and we've acquired new skills and understandings along the way. Yet, we have a choice about how we show up in life each day and in every situation. The key is to do this consciously, so that you are being who you want to be.

EXERCISE: LIST THE INHERENT TRAITS WITH WHICH YOU WERE BORN, YOUR TRUE-SPIRITED NATURE, THE THINGS AND ACTIVITIES TO WHICH YOU ARE NATURALLY DRAWN.

LIST THE SKILLS, ABILITIES AND TALENTS YOU ACQUIRED ALONG THE WAY, THEN SHORTEN THAT LIST TO THE THINGS YOU ARE REALLY GOOD AT AND GENUINELY ENJOY.

LIST THE QUALITIES IN OTHERS THAT YOU ADMIRE.

LIST THE THINGS THAT ARE IMPORTANT TO YOU – YOUR VALUES.

NOW, BEING REALISTIC ABOUT WHO YOU REALLY ARE, YET MINDFUL OF THE PERSON YOU ARE WILLING TO PUT THE EFFORT INTO BECOMING, SELECT THE MOST MEANINGFUL ASPECTS OF THE ABOVE TO MAP OUT THE PERSON YOU CHOOSE TO BE.

BE – DO – HAVE

You should now have a clearer take on who you are and what you want to be. A common framework to use is the BE – DO – HAVE model. The key with this model is that it specifies the order in which these should be prioritized, BE – DO – HAVE. We are conditioned to believe we will be happy and fulfilled when we HAVE the promotion, car, house, holiday, branded clothing and so on, because that drives the wheels of industry. The problem with this is that there is always something more to aim for, as the initial satisfaction of attainment is normally short-lived, so a new goal is set and the hamster-wheel existence is set in motion. When we focus first on the most important thing, on how we want to BE (authentically) and DO the things we want to do, the HAVE part becomes less important and life defining.

BE

How do you want to BE in life? How do you want to show up? Relaxed or pumped up, hands on or hands off? Very physically fit, or a couch potato? Always learning new things or sticking to an established routine? There are no wrong answers here. Be careful not to slip into judgment, remember it is about what is important to you. It would be great to have all the positive attributes in spades, but the reality is that if, for example, you want to be exceedingly fit, the time, effort and dedication required to become so will mean sacrificing other important things in your life. So maybe you want to be reasonably fit, doing activities you enjoy with other people to help you attain and maintain that?

What are your values? What are the things or ways of being that are most important to you, the things you respect and admire in others? Or perhaps it may be easier to see the traits that you dislike most in others and practise the opposite.

What are your behavioural traits? How are you with yourself and how are you with others? Are you organized and planned or are you last minute and spontaneous? Are you anxious or calm, the life and soul of the party, or the person who likes to help out in the background?

Track these preferences, and any others that come to mind that are important to you, look at the way you show up – is it the way you want to show up? How would you like to be now and in the short term; in other words, how could you change the way you show up in the short term? How would you like to be in the future; in other words, what is the direction you want to move towards in the longer term? That will take more time and effort to achieve.

DO

What are the things you are good at? What do you enjoy doing? What do you wish you could do more of? What do you wish you could do less of?

What are the things you do that add the most value to yourself or others? What would you need to do and how can you do more of the things that deliver value to your life?

Effectiveness first. Before you even consider looking at time management or anything like that, what are the things that you do that are most effective, the things that generate enjoyment, satisfaction and results? These are the things to get clear and on which to focus. What can you change now, what can you do in the future?

Efficiency second. Now that you are clearer about how you want to be, and what you want to do, it's time to start looking at being more efficient with your time. Do you have an early morning routine to set yourself up for the rest of the day? Do you set clear plans and goals for the day, week, month, quarter, year ahead and further ahead? Do you put aside time for you in the schedule? Do you allow for flexibility and downtime so you don't beat yourself up if the relentless list is not fully completed?

HAVE

What do you want to have? Time, money, things, experiences? Personally, I'm not a great fan of the vision board or mood board full of Caribbean holidays, nice houses and cars that are meant to motivate you to take action now so you can attain these things down the line. Having said that, having some idea of what you want can give you direction and focus. It can be more interesting, however, to ask yourself what is the underlying need you seek to fulfill from having those things, and how that feeling could be gained sooner, without acquiring that end goal?

For example, if you'd like to have a lot of money, there is a good chance that you are looking for greater financial security. The mere fact that you are doing what you are doing right now – reading this book – means that, one way or another, you have survived financially thus far. Fortunately, in the Western world, few of us fear having no food or shelter, our basic survival needs are met by the safety net of the welfare state (it may not be perfect – but massively better than nothing!) So, by recognizing that you have survived financially this far, how could you tap into, and trust, that you will do what is necessary to secure your financial needs going forward? The better you become at tapping into this feeling now, the less you will experience the sense of lack that drives the need to acquire more money in the future. This will allow you to feel more secure in the present, which means you can show up (BE) in a less fearful way, which frees you up to DO things better, and consequently you'll come through HAVING more in any event!

3. ATTITUDE

"YOUR ATTITUDE, NOT YOUR APTITUDE,
WILL DETERMINE YOUR ALTITUDE"
(Zig Ziglar)

Attitudes stem from your beliefs. The big, determining belief that will affect the quality of your success in all domains is whether you believe that life is something that happens to you (and allow yourself to be sucked into the blame and victim culture encouraged by the media) or whether you believe you are responsible for your own life, attitudes and responses. If you believe the latter, and the fact that you are reading a book such as this suggests you do, then a richer world awaits you as you develop the attitudes that will help you along your way.

When I look back, there are certain traits and particular attitudes that helped me build two multi-million-pound businesses and recover from a serious car accident in between. These include: a 'can-do' attitude, determination, single-mindedness, resilience, belief, thinking big, clinical decision-making, passion, enthusiasm, focus, honesty and straight talking. But I also worked as part of a team in which other people's attitudes balanced mine, so the list of attitudes is not universal. Display attitudes that are important to you, not just those that are perceived to be right.

One way to help foster unstoppable belief is to set the right foundations for your life and work. In so doing, you get to focus on the few things that are important to you and take relentless action around them. As you reinforce the belief and the action in the same areas of your life, you cannot stop the inevitable upward spiral. The HARMONY model outlined later in this book will help you to achieve this.

EXERCISE: WHAT ATTITUDES TO LIFE DO YOU BRING WITH YOU, NATURALLY? LIST THEM, OWN THEM!

WHEN I LOOK AT SOME OF THE ATTITUDES I'VE LEARNED SINCE DEALING WITH SIGNIFICANT SETBACKS, AND WHICH HAVE HELPED ME BECOME A MORE ROUNDED PERSON, THESE INCLUDE COMPASSION, KINDNESS, GENEROSITY OF SPIRIT, OPEN-HEARTEDNESS AND TRUST.

EXERCISE: WHICH OF THE COLLECTION OF TRAITS AND ATTITUDES THAT YOU HAVE WOULD YOU LIKE TO DROP OR ALTER?

WHAT TRAITS AND ATTITUDES WOULD YOU LIKE DEVELOP TO GIVE YOU A MORE ROUNDED CAPABILITY?

4. AWARENESS

Awareness is a fundamental foundation stone for any endeavour. Imagine driving a car with the windscreen totally frosted up, and just a small space cleared through which to see. How can you possibly be aware of what is going on around you so you can chose your response accordingly?

5. SELF-AWARENESS

We go about our daily lives largely by routine and habit. We expect others around us to behave in certain ways, and get into a pattern of responding to them in a way that is mostly instinctive, reactive and without thought.

"What's wrong with that?" you may well ask. "Isn't that normal?"
Yes it is very normal; in fact, I'd confidently say that most people live their lives like that. The problem with this way of being, is that it becomes very easy to get wrapped up in stories and dramas in our minds that run over and over again. Spend a little time in a shopping mall and listen to the passing conversations. I often witness people sharing with a friend the frustrations they have had with another person, or situations that weren't their fault, and how so-and-so has been unreasonable and why they do what they do, it's just not fair, and so forth.

The details are always different but the essence of the conversation is that external circumstances have made their life harder. Two things happen when we do this: we fill our minds with a ranty story, that we repeat often, and we shift the focus of attention away from ourselves and on to the external issue. This cycle becomes repetitive, reinforcing, and disempowering.

MIND TALK

If we want to lead an authentic and successful life, truer to our own deepest longings, we need to quieten the endless chatter, rumination and blame that can occupy our minds.

It is difficult to make any meaningful changes to how the mind operates. If it were easy, we could all have an instruction manual, read, digest and understand – and "hey presto!" we'd be sorted! If only it could be that simple.

So be wary of any instant breakthrough formula, system or experience. I've tried and tested a good many of these, only to find the result is a great short-term experience, but little in the way of lasting change. More commonly, these experiences lead to increased personal discomfort as I'm made aware of a bigger, better, brighter place out there, yet find myself in the same place as previously. While we can definitely stand on the shoulders of others (as Sir Isaac Newton once said) and learn from their experiences, we still need to find our own way that makes sense to us and resonates with the way we want to show up in life.

We are far more intelligent than just our minds: a friend of mine, following a horse-riding accident, had to have a significant muscle transplant in her leg. When fully recovered, she found she couldn't ride a horse properly as the new muscle didn't have the intelligence to ride. The mind knew what to do but the stored muscle memory was simply not there, so she had to learn over again. Bruce Lipton in his book *The Biology of Belief* explains how intelligence is at the membrane of the cell, and not in the nucleus as we are all taught in school. And Einstein reminds us we cannot solve problems by using the same kind of thinking we used to create them. So in order to gain greater clarity and insight, we need to get out of our minds and into our bodies.

How often have you had great insight into a problem you've been pondering when in the shower, walking the dog or during a long drive? I've noticed this is quite a common experience for many of us. The reason is that during these activities we're preoccupied with a familiar activity that doesn't require a lot of thought, we are free from distraction, and our mind doesn't think it needs to be working something out, so naturally it quietens down. It's when the mind settles in this way that insights occur.

When writing this text, as soon as I get wrapped up in the mind, the thoughts and fears develop about what to say or how to express it, whether it will make sense, whether it will be "good enough". When this happens, I have a strong urge to find a displacement activity: make a cup of tea, check emails, play solitaire and so on. Yet when I manage to still my mind and sit with the discomfort, I begin to experience it as simple body sensations rather than a scary movie generated by a stream of thoughts. I am able to face the fear, move through it to the other side and write another paragraph or two.

But why wait for random insights in the shower? And beware (be-aware): as soon as you start expecting insights in the shower, they dry up! Practising mindfulness is worth the effort. Like anything, you can work at this at different levels; for starters, the old adage we learned as a child, to count to ten, can be invaluable.

On one occasion several years ago, I was having an extremely challenging conversation, and at one point, was about to burst into a fit of rage, I had less awareness of, and insight into, my thoughts and emotions then, so I forced myself to focus, by closing my eyes and counting to ten. The other person was somewhat surprised, but it gave both of us the space to come back from the brink. The essence is in the power of taking time out, taking a pause. In fact, there is an organization that believes the path to enlightenment is through repeatedly taking pauses, or "short moments" as they call them (see balancedview.org).

BREATHING

Another part of pausing is breathing. When we become fearful or concerned we naturally contract and our breathing becomes higher in the chest and shallower. By taking a few deeper breaths, we naturally tell the body that it's ok. In fact, it has been shown that if you exhale for longer than you inhale, this has a natural calming effect on the body and the mind.

One approach (outlined in Joe Griffin and Ivan Tyrrell's book, *Human givens: a new approach to emotional health and clear thinking*) is to breathe in to the count of seven and breathe out to the count of 11.

If that is too much of a stretch, change the numbers to five and eight, for example. Try it right now, for at least five cycles, and notice what happens. It works best if you close your eyes, breathe in through your nose and breathe out through your mouth.

So how was that? Did you try it? If not, take a couple of minutes to experience this. Remember, you won't get much out of this book simply by reading it. Did you find it easy to drop into your body and let your mind settle, or did you notice your mind running off on a story – about how silly this exercise is, for example?

The great thing about the breath is that it is something we have with us all the time, and by turning attention to breathing we can bring ourselves back into our body and re-centre. Whether this is when stuck in traffic, on the tube, or during a restless night's sleep, simply reconnecting with the breath, and remembering to breathe slowly and deeply, can be surprisingly helpful. Like this, many of the suggestions you will find in this book are very simple and easy to do. But, don't be fooled into thinking they are too simple, subconsciously discouraging yourself from putting in the effort to practise them regularly.

MINDFULNESS

To take this breath work further, I'd strongly recommend developing a meditation habit. Through this practice, you learn to notice and observe what is going on in your mind and your body. The key is to resist the temptation to judge, criticise and fix what you notice! What we resist persists, and it is through resisting 'what is' that most of our pain and suffering comes.

Imagine your thoughts as clouds in the sky; the clear blue expanse of the open sky is always there (just remember when you last went up in an aeroplane) and thoughts come and go. When we get caught up in our thoughts, we feel consumed by them and unable to see the clear blue sky beyond. When we rest in awareness, we become more comfortable letting thoughts come and go without getting drawn into them, we can see them from the perspective of the vast open space of the clear blue sky.

Through persistent meditation practice we grow to understand, and eventually experience, that what is happening doesn't actually matter that much; what matters is how we relate to the event. Nelson Mandela's autobiography *The Long Walk to Freedom*, and Viktor Frankl's *Man's Search for Meaning*, both demonstrate the power of this concept in extreme circumstances, so we know it's possible in everyday life. The best book I've found on the power of mindfulness is *Radical Acceptance: Awakening the love that heals fear and shame*, by Tara Brach. To help with daily meditation practice, there is a great app available, via headspace.com

PERSONAL GPS

Without going down a formal meditation path, you should at least take a few moments out of the day to sit still, close your eyes, take a few deep breaths, and check in with your body. What are your thoughts? Just notice what they are about, without judgment, without getting sucked into them.

What are your bodily sensations? Where is your body relaxed? Where are tension spots? Scan your whole body from head-to-toe and just accept what you notice, without trying to change anything. Breathe into the sensations and question what they are trying to tell you.

What emotions are you experiencing? How are you feeling, are there lots of feelings or just one dominant feeling? Again, just accept these as they are, just notice them. What is your general vibe or energy level like, are you feeling alive and radiant, or small and deflated? Just note this. And as you notice, with increasing ease and curiosity, ask your intuition what message it has for you, what is your intention and longing right now?

In this way, reconnecting with your body and your senses becomes your personal GPS system. It reads all the instruments we have at hand and reminds us to get back on course. It's a powerful tool, and like all things, it takes time to practise and to perfect, but over time you'll wonder why you haven't used it before to read situations and to adjust course more naturally and skilfully. This is far better than being stuck in the head, feeling stressed, and only recognizing this once we've begun to experience severe back ache, or a headache and sought help from a doctor!

If meditation really isn't your thing, try other activities that quieten your mind and encourage you to be fully present in the body; for example, running, cycling, yoga, dance, music, martial arts and so on. But try and listen to your whole body and not just your mind. In this way, your mind gets a rest, it doesn't have to solve everything alone, and after this rest, it will be refreshed and able to leap into action when you call on it the next time.

6. AWARENESS IN RELATIONSHIPS

Knowing yourself, being able to still the mind and track your thoughts, emotions, body, energy and intuition as a guiding GPS is great, and in my opinion essential. But when we interact with others, that's when the rubber hits the road. From time to time, we come across people who piss us off, to put it bluntly. It's very easy to say they caused us pain, and from that space, it is very easy to slide into blame mode, they were wrong and you were right to raise your self-righteous hackles and condemn them for their behaviour. It's what our political leaders have been doing for centuries, leading us into countless wars.

What a waste. It's rarely an effective way to carry on.

As with the self-awareness described above, when we accept what is happening simply "as it is" we give ourselves the space to choose a response, rather than reacting to it blindly. It is important to note here that acceptance doesn't mean being a doormat, it means not resisting. Remember, what we resist persists and the cycle is locked in to repeat itself.

When we accept things as they are, without the inherent suffering that arises when we resist, it gives us space to see more clearly. We can then allow ourselves more freedom to choose how we want to respond. It is the judgment that we make about a person or an event that determines how we feel, and in turn, how we react and respond.

Typically, when confronted, we respond in aggressive or defensive ways if we allow ourselves to react from a place of fear. If we are able to give ourselves a little space to consider what the other person must be going through to behave in that way, it gives us greater flexibility to respond in a more understanding way. This can give rise to a path leading to resolution rather than confrontation.

If we let ourselves continue being annoyed with someone for a period of time, resentment kicks in. The best way I've heard resentment described is as setting yourself on fire and expecting the other person to be hurt. It simply doesn't work; seething with rage about someone, or past wrongs, when the person is no longer there to communicate directly is pointless. Yet that doesn't stop us from being easily drawn into this very human and understandable behaviour. Often, the prescribed remedy for resentment is forgiveness, but this may lead to the feeling that somebody has been let off the hook. For many people this feels plain wrong.

My take on it is more pragmatic. The first step is acceptance again, what is done is done, history can't be re-written, but its interpretation most definitely can be re-written. If you look back at all the hard times you've had, no matter how bad they were, my bet is that you will, with hindsight, be able to see how you've grown stronger, wiser or more capable as a result of the experience.

When we learn to view things this way, we can start the challenging but worthwhile process of learning to be grateful for the benefits we have gained from enduring hard times. This way, it doesn't let the other person off the hook, it frees us from the resentment, and allows us to draw strength from the experience and to move on quicker, without a bitter heart. I've tried this (more times than I'd like to have had to) and it does work.

EXAMPLE: I WAS WORKING WITH A YOUNG COUPLE, LET'S CALL THEM MIKE AND MANDY; MANDY WAS PREGNANT WITH MIKE'S CHILD. MANDY HAD RECENTLY REVEALED THAT SOME OF HER BEHAVIOURS HAD INVOLVED SLEEPING WITH EXES, IN ADDITION TO THE DRUG AND ALCOHOL USE OF WHICH MIKE WAS ALREADY AWARE.

THIS PUT THE RELATIONSHIP UNDER SIGNIFICANT STRAIN, TO THE REAL PROSPECT OF IRRETRIEVABLE BREAKDOWN. TALKING THROUGH THE ISSUES WITH THEM, I HELPED THEM LEARN A DIFFERENT STYLE OF COMMUNICATING WITH EACH OTHER, BECOMING MORE AWARE OF WHAT WAS GOING ON FOR EACH OTHER, AND BETWEEN THEM, AS A COUPLE.

SPECIFICALLY, I SHOWED THEM SIMPLE WAYS TO 'TIME OUT' DURING THE CONVERSATION, IN REAL TIME, AS THINGS BEGAN TO GROW HEATED, AND HOW TO DO THIS REPEATEDLY, SO THE CONVERSATION COULD CONTINUE.

MANDY WAS ENCOURAGED TO EXPLORE WHAT WAS ACTUALLY HAPPENING WITH HER THOUGHTS, FEELINGS AND BODILY SENSATIONS AS SHE MADE THE INSTINCTIVE DECISION TO WITHDRAW FROM THE CONVERSATION WHEN IT GOT UNCOMFORTABLE. IN THIS WAY, THE ISSUES COULD ACTUALLY GET DISCUSSED.

MANDY BECAME AWARE OF THE LANGUAGE SHE USED AND
SHE NOTICED THAT, OFTEN, WHAT SHE HAD SAID AT THE TIME
WAS NOT WHAT SHE ACTUALLY MEANT.

MIKE REALISED THAT, AS HE BECAME ANGRIER, HIS SPEECH
GREW FASTER, AND BECAME MORE ACCUSATORY IN TONE
AND DELIVERY. WHILE THIS WAS UNDERSTANDABLE, IT WAS
REALLY UNHELPFUL IN TERMS OF FINDING A WAY FORWARD,
AS IT MERELY LOCKED THE SITUATION INTO CYCLES OF ATTACK
AND DEFEND.

BOTH, MIKE AND MANDY LEARNED THAT SIMPLY MIRRORING
BACK WHAT THE OTHER PERSON HAD SAID, WITHOUT JUDGMENT,
COMMENT OR DEFENCE, ALLOWED THE OTHER PERSON TO FEEL
HEARD. AT THE SAME TIME, THIS APPROACH SLOWED DOWN THE
CONVERSATION SO THAT REACTIVE RESPONSES WERE LESS
LIKELY TO BE FIRED OFF.

THEY WERE INTRODUCED TO THE CONCEPT OF OWNING
THEIR BEHAVIOURS AND RECOGNIZING THE IMPACT THOSE
BEHAVIOURS HAD ON THE OTHER PERSON, WITHOUT BEING
TEMPTED TO HIDE BEHIND EXCUSES OR BLAME.

I WAS ABLE TO EXPLAIN TO THEM THAT WHILE THEY FELT A HUGE
TIME PRESSURE TO RESOLVE THEIR ISSUES BECAUSE OF
HOUSING AND PREGNANCY NEEDS, THE EXTRA PRESSURE WAS

COMPOUNDING THE PROBLEM. BY SLOWING DOWN AND GIVING THEMSELVES TIME AND SPACE, THEY WOULD ACTUALLY SPEED UP THE WHOLE PROCESS. THROUGH EASING BACK A LITTLE AND USING SIMPLE COMMUNICATION TECHNIQUES, THEY WERE ABLE TO CREATE A NEW SPACE IN WHICH TO WORK, WHERE THERE WAS A MUCH GREATER LIKELIHOOD OF RESOLUTION.

I ASKED THEM TO CONSIDER APPROACHING THEIR DEADLOCK WITH SMALL, SIMPLE STEPS, RATHER THAN LOOKING FOR THE ONE BIG GESTURE/MAGIC WAND TO SOLVE IT; FOR EXAMPLE, JUST HOLDING HANDS AND LOOKING INTO EACH OTHER'S EYES WITHOUT SPEAKING FOR A SHORT WHILE. AND SLOWLY TAKING STEPS TO COME BACK FROM THE BRINK AND TO REMEMBER THEY WERE BOTH TENDER, HURT YOUNG BEINGS AT HEART.

AS A RESULT OF THIS, THEY WERE ABLE TO WORK THROUGH THEIR CHALLENGES AND WENT ON TO BUILD A FULFILLING RELATIONSHIP TOGETHER.

7. AWARENESS AT WORK

How often do you walk or drive down a familiar street and not notice what is around you? Part of being alive, fully alive, is being aware of what is going on around us. To notice the beauty that is right in front of us, the things going on and so forth. It triggers a sense of wonder and curiosity and, if nothing else, it is a lot of fun!

In business, I have found much of the impact I've made is simply through sitting back and observing what's going on, regularly and repeatedly; what works, what doesn't work, where patterns are emerging, what the likely consequences of following a particular path may be. Try it and see.

Take time out to step back and observe what's going on – practical solutions will appear, and afterwards these may seem obvious. The reason these things were not so obvious beforehand is there are so many competing options and day-to-day pressing demands that we miss what is right in front of us.

It becomes obvious with hindsight, because it just makes sense. The reason these solutions are relatively rare is because many of us are so busy doing what we're doing, we don't spend time looking around, just to watch, listen and absorb.

In the workplace, there are multiple things of which to be aware in the wider environment including political, economic, social, technological, environmental and legal changes.

From your industry: the trends, the competition, the new entrants, fashion changes.

From your particular workplace: sales, marketing, operations, staff, customers, suppliers, finances, performance tracking and so on.

And then from the daily interactions with colleagues, bosses, customers, suppliers and so on.

In each area, take time out to step back every now and then, to see what is happening objectively and with a beginner's mind. You are certain to notice new things and gain valuable insights.

8. ACCEPTANCE

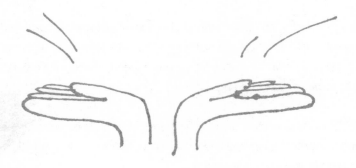

"WHAT WE RESIST PERSISTS"
(Carl Jung)

We all naturally want to improve things and to have life rearrange itself so that it is more convenient and allows us to enjoy things the way we want them to be. The problem is that in feeling this way we resist 'what is' (lack of acceptance) and so generate internal frustration, which is rarely helpful in bringing about the changes we seek. Paradoxically, learning to accept 'what is' is one of the great levers of change. In this section, we look at acceptance from three different perspectives, mental, physical and total.

9. MENTAL ACCEPTANCE

On a straightforward, or thinking, level, accepting 'what is', is plain and simple logic. It is what it is. Whether we choose to try and do something about it or not is a different matter that we'll look at later, but before the rush to resist or change 'what is', consider accepting 'what is'. It may seem absurdly simple and obvious, but in most cases nothing could be further from the truth.

When someone irritates us, the suffering (as Buddhists would call it) in the irritation is caused not by the actions or behaviour of the other person, but our resistance, non-acceptance or plain rejection of their behaviour.

In the nanosecond between an event, trigger or stimulus of some sort, most of us instinctively (that is, without thought or consideration) make a judgment about what has occurred. The judgment creates a feeling within us and from that feeling we generate our reaction, which again is instinctive.

TRIGGER > JUDGMENT > FEELING > REACTION

When we learn to create a small space between the trigger and the judgment, we give ourselves the chance to choose our response, rather than being led by our instinctive reactions which are based on past (often unhelpful) conditioning.

TRIGGER > PAUSE > ACCEPTANCE > ASSESSMENT
> DISCERNMENT > FEELING > RESPONSE

It may look like a whole lot more steps, but in reality these things happen at speed. It may take practice to pause, consciously, before blowing up, but it really is worth the effort to gradually build up mastery of this practice. When you do, your happiness will no longer be dependent on how others behave.

Let's look at an example: you return home from work, tired and possibly a little distracted. Your partner goes off on a rant because you've failed to pick up the milk from the store on the way home.

Old pattern scenario:

"Jeeez!" is your reaction. "How many times have I remembered the milk, done this, that and the other, don't you know I've had a hard day, it just slipped my mind. Why do expect me to be perfect all the time? I'm never good enough in your eyes, you are impossible to please." This flurry of thoughts happens almost instantaneously. The judgment is that your partner is being unreasonable.

You feel annoyed because it's not fair and you feel you can never win. You react with a heavy sigh and snap back with a retort about something they've forgotten, so now you both feel miserable, and despite going back to get the milk, the damage has been done, and you can cut the atmosphere with a knife.

New pattern scenario:

You take a breath. Pause. "My partner is unhappy, that's ok, I don't need to fix it, reject it or argue with it (acceptance). What's going on here? I forgot the milk, this is true (acceptance again, and no need to go into a story or drama about why that is). You apologize for forgetting the milk, ask if anything else has caused concern, and listen openly to the response (assessment). I recognize my partner has had a challenging day, and that my forgetfulness was the proverbial straw that broke the camel's back (discernment). I show empathy and understanding for the situations that have arisen, with as much compassion as I can muster in the moment (feeling), and agree to return to buy the milk and a couple of other things that we need while I'm at it (response).

Outcome: the situation is resolved without further escalation, and the likelihood of continuing the evening in better humour has greatly increased. Did it take much longer? Probably not, as the spiralling, compounding dynamic from the normal approach of the old pattern lasts for hours, days and beyond, and each minor hiccup along the way simply builds on this unhelpful foundation.

EXERCISE

IN WHAT AREA OF YOUR LIFE DO YOU FIND YOURSELF CONSISTENTLY LOCKED INTO A SIMILAR REPEATING DYNAMIC?

TRIGGER > PAUSE > ACCEPTANCE > ASSESSMENT > DISCERNMENT > FEELING > RESPONSE

EXPERIMENT WITH THE ABOVE APPROACH AND SEE WHAT CHANGES FOR YOU.

10. PHYSICAL ACCEPTANCE

The long dark nights!....

So, mastering acceptance in relation to other people and events is pretty handy when you encounter the next traffic jam, irate customer or grumpy teenager, but what about the long, dark nights? Do you ever have those? When a collection of thoughts runs and runs and runs and runs. No matter how hard you try to stop them they keep on running? There have been times in my life when I've had such significant experiences of this that I have given it my full attention and research.

This is my experience. The thoughts tend to come in one of two flavours: agonizing over the loss of something that I previously had (relationships, assets, status and so on) or worrying about an upcoming doomsday scenario that is so catastrophic that my life as I know it is going to change irrevocably for the worse, yet I feel powerless to do anything about it.

Neuroscience tells us that as we create thoughts and replay them, we create new synaptic pathways, which make it easier for the same thought process to run down. It's a bit like taking a fresh green field, and as you create the thought it leaves a trail in the grass, as you repeat the thought process it becomes a pathway, and after a few sleepless nights you've created a full blown six-lane superhighway for the thought pattern to access and run down. There are four points to bear in mind here:

1. Be careful what thoughts you choose
2. When you notice unhelpful thoughts, the earlier you take corrective action, the easier it will become
3. If you have a full-blown super highway running with unhelpful thoughts, you'd probably best get some help to decommission it
4. Know that you are ultimately responsible for the thoughts you entertain in your personal house.

So, in the meantime, what do you do when you are tossing and turning through the night resisting the urge to get up and watch the telly, read a book or see who else is on facebook?

In fact, it can be radically simple, though like most simple things, it takes practice and perseverance. The practice is this: when the recurring unpleasant thought occurs, rest with it, and ask yourself where are you physically feeling the discomfort of the unpleasant thought. It physically manifests somewhere in your body. When you've located the feeling, bring your attention to that place and purposefully and steadily breathe into it. Breathe with deep, stable breaths, feel your breath enter all the way down to the base of your spine, and breathe out steadily with the location of the physical pain at the centre of your attention.

As you do this you will probably notice two things: first, you'll be distracted by the original thought pattern and grow frustrated, and second, the location of the physical feeling moves from place to place. Both of these are normal and to be expected. The next stage is the same, regardless, to return to the exercise of focusing your steady breath on the physical location. Do it over and over and over again, in a similar way to returning to the breath when learning to meditate.

It is worth it, because as you focus on the physical sensation you'll feel it dissipate, all by itself, as if by magic, and a sense of calm will return to the body and the mind. Sure, it doesn't last, but you are breaking the habit of creating the neural superhighway in your mind, while simultaneously experiencing significant pain relief and getting some sleep. It really is worth it!

EXERCISE: TRY IT!

11. TOTAL ACCEPTANCE

Though physical acceptance works well, there is a catch – ultimately it is a hack, you do it because it helps alleviate the pain of unpleasant thoughts. By focusing on the physical sensation, you know the discomfort will go away, which means the original intent is non-acceptance!

So now what? Total acceptance...

Do you ever have a nagging inner voice, an inner critic if you will, who seems to know best; the Smart Alec on the sidelines who berates, sighs, and chastises you?

If mastering mental acceptance helps you deal mentally with external events, and mastering physical acceptance helps deal with sleepless nights physically, how do you handle the persistent inner critic?

This is where total acceptance comes in. One way of looking at ourselves is as many parts or characters. Each of us houses a whole family of different characters, and each character has different roles and responsibilities. Each of these characters has developed strategies to help us on our way. The challenge is that many of these strategies developed when we were small children and are less helpful now that we have grown into adults.

If you are anything like me, you will have disliked the 'unhelpful' parts of yourself; the characters within you who make you feel unconfident, shy, who allow you to procrastinate and then beat yourself up for doing so, and so on. In disliking characters within me, I effectively resist them, and of course, what we resist persists.

I had a profound experience following my car accident, where the physical pain grew so intense, despite all the opiates, distraction and displacement activities that I'd come to use as pain management, that I was literally forced to turn, face and embrace the pain. This is not an easy thing to do, it is so counterintuitive, and I was led to an extreme situation in order to go there, but when I did, the effect was transformational. When I turned, faced and embraced the pain, totally and whole-heartedly, I transcended it, it was as if I had travelled through the pain to the other side, to a different place where the pain was demonstrably more bearable.

The good news is that this very same principle can be applied to different areas of our lives. So, using a much more mundane example to illustrate this point, I recently took up 'five rhythms' dancing. As a guy who considers himself to be untrendy, with two left feet, one arm and no rhythm, there was no shortage of stories running in my head creating fears of embarrassment. So I decided to play with 'turning, facing and embracing' those frightened, child-like characters within me. To do so, I had to create a kind, loving nurturing parent-like character within me to embrace, accept and listen to the frightened parts inside. What happened next can only be described as magical! To create the caring, parent-like character within me, I had, in effect, to grow myself. As I embraced the frightened parts, they suddenly eased and relaxed; for the first time they were not being pushed away, feeling unwanted. With the combination of simultaneously relaxing and growing, I couldn't wipe the grin off my face for a full 15 minutes, and have danced more confidently and gracefully ever since!

This approach can be developed with an "I'm sorry, please forgive me, thank you and I love you" format. In this way, your loving parent character apologizes to the child part for not accepting it, then asks for forgiveness for being so stern. In recognizing that the frightened part has been trying to protect your core essence from past patterns, thanks – and ultimately love – is given to both the child-like part and the essence it was trying to protect.

Following on from this, you can choose a more constructive path forward with fewer constraints from the past.

EXERCISE: RINSE AND REPEAT FREQUENTLY!

12. APPRECIATION

"WHAT WE APPRECIATE, APPRECIATES"

It's so easy to become wrapped up in our worries about the future and all the things we don't have that we forget how far we have come and what we do have.

It's a truism that we get more of what we focus on. That's why happier, more optimistic people tend to experience happier lives, and depressed people tend to drift in and out of that state, because they have both built habits on what they focus on. The results are self-fulfilling.

So, the more we appreciate what we are, what we do and what we have, the more we actually appreciate them. In other words, what we appreciate appreciates!

Being appreciated is one of the most seductive feelings we have, we just love it. But we are not in control of whether we are appreciated. Sure, we can do helpful things for other people, but if we do that in expectation of appreciation, that neediness leaks out and spoils the giving. Being of service, without expecting anything in return, is certainly a path to happiness, because it shifts attention from our own worries and fears, towards constructively supporting others. But in practice, this is far more easily said than done. More often than not, there is score-keeping going on in the background, a metaphorical bank account of transactions, and a sense of resentment or entitlement develops if the bank balance goes too far into the red.

The 'trick' is to learn to appreciate ourselves. We can use the trigger of yearning for external validation, or appreciation, from others to remind us that we have that appreciation feeling already within us, and that when we appreciate ourselves we can access it. When this is practised, we can be of service to others without the need for recognition, appreciation and praise, which means we can give without expectation. Paradoxically, of course, when we give without expectation, we are more likely to receive the appreciation we no longer need, but can now gracefully receive and appreciate!

So being aware of ourselves allows us to learn to respond in the way we choose to, rather than being at the mercy of our instinctive reactions. Accepting ourselves opens the doorway to letting go of the need to control and beat ourselves up. Appreciation allows us to come from a place of genuine, loving kindness, and that opens up an entire new world to explore and enjoy.

EXERCISE: KEEP A GRATITUDE JOURNAL, MAKE A NOTE OF AT LEAST THREE THINGS FOR WHICH YOU ARE GRATEFUL EACH NIGHT BEFORE YOU GO TO BED.

13. ATTACHMENT

"WHEN WE FREE OURSELVES UP FROM WORRYING ABOUT THE OUTCOME, WE CAN FOCUS MORE ON OUR APPROACH AND ALLOW THE OUTCOME TO LOOK AFTER ITSELF"
(Tim Johnson)

Buddhists teach that suffering comes from our attachment to things, and wanting things to remain as they are. They believe in a world of impermanence, of constant change, that holding on to things and expecting them to stay the same is madness. Moreover, by expecting things to stay the same, we not only set ourselves up for disappointment but lose the ability to appreciate what we have, and are experiencing, in the present moment. By expecting things, we forget that this particular moment will never be exactly the same again. Never. Each moment is uniquely different, and when we remember this and tap into it, we remember how wonderful and magnificent it is to be alive.

In a world which is predicated on striving to achieve things, and acquiring possessions and relationships, it seems almost heretical to suggest that we should not be attached to the things to which we have given so much importance, and by which we might even have been defined.

My personal take on this is borne from both from wrestling, intellectually, with the conflicting elements of this principle, and from having to deal with my own direct experience. In a literal sense, I was attached to my arm, it was part of me, it was mine, my arm. And yet when the surgeon amputated it because the damage was beyond repair, it was gone. It was physically detached (yet the phantom sensation of my hand still rests in my stump to this day). I was lucky, because I had anticipated losing the whole arm, not just half of it, and the battle to save the upper arm took two years.

So the combination of a better-than-expected outcome, and the distractive focus of a two-year healing journey, helped reduce my sense of grief at the loss of my arm. Notice also how my choosing to frame it that way helped manage the letting go of the attachment. Yet the fact remains that I lost my arm, to which I was physically and emotionally attached, I experienced excruciating pain and still experience regular low-level pain to this day. (I was going to write that I still experience permanent low-level pain, but being more mindful, particularly when writing a piece about impermanence, I realized that my truth is that the pain in my stump is variable and not permanent.)

When it's gone it's gone! I found I was drawn to make a conscious choice: did I want to sink or swim? There was no point in wallowing in the dark pit of self pity, flailing about in the murky and muddy swamp, spreading muck all around me. It was exhausting and unpleasant. I could either let the swamp envelop me and rest there, or choose to head for the nearest thing that looked like firm ground and take baby steps in that direction.

By literally, mentally and emotionally letting go of my arm (that is, dropping all attachment) I was able to move on. As I've moved on I've been taken to places deep inside myself that have deepened my resilience. I've had richer and more meaningful experiences that have enabled me to connect with people in a more humourous and disarming way. It is because of this that I am now able to say that the journey since the accident has more than made up for the loss of my arm.

When we lose things we've previously held dear, it takes us to places inside that we'd rather not visit. At the time of writing this book, I've experienced a whole year of letting go and learning to drop a host of things that most of us have, or aspire to have: I separated from my wife and family, leaving behind the nice big house and my position within that community, moving 40 miles away to a rented flat in Bristol, where I knew few people (although I soon realized I brought myself with me – but that's another story!). I had three business projects that were set to develop into a nice portfolio and, for different reasons, they all faded away. I fell truly, madly, deeply for a new woman (six months after separation), only for the relationship to be short-lived.

So I lost money, assets, identity, hope, friends, relationships, status and standing. It was not pleasant. Many dark nights of abject terror were indeed endured. And yet, through that journey, I've come to love and accept myself at the core, without the shields of success behind which I used to hide. I've come to face my fears head on and work through them (not always gracefully!) so that I am now much more self-assured, more loving and less fearful than previously. It is a journey, and can be a lifetime's work, this stuff!

This is not to say that we should forsake all worldly goods and sit on a mountain top in a monastery (although if that's your calling, go and do it). I have the wish and desire to go on to create much value for others, to build a wealth of time, money, experiences and relationships and to truly enjoy them.

Be careful not to imagine a pedestal version of yourself, that is frankly unachievable and the source of frustration and procrastination, from which I still suffer. We are multi-faceted beings and it is only when we embrace ourselves, warts and all, that we set ourselves free to experience life in full broadband. You must be able to care deeply, while not getting attached to way things turn out, because what happens happens. When it does, even if the proverbial shit hits the fan, you will have the resources to deal with it one way or another, and the quality of your experience will be largely determined by your ability to let go of your attachment. If we embrace all the new feelings and experiences that come with it, feelings of loss, sorrow, grief and so on, let them come, embrace them, own them, welcome them and let them in, they'll pass on through to the other side and be dealt with, rather than hanging around as baggage. Not easy, but worth it!

EXERCISE: WHAT ARE YOU HOLDING ONTO THAT LETTING GO WOULD SET YOU FREE?

14. ALIGNMENT

> **"THE COMMON EYE SEES ONLY THE OUTSIDE OF THINGS, AND JUDGES BY THAT, BUT THE SEEING EYE PIERCES THROUGH AND READS THE HEART AND THE SOUL"**
> (Mark Twain)

The brain is an amazing tool. We can plan, we can organize, prioritize, assess, evaluate, learn, work things out, think of new possibilities, rationalize, objectify and so on. It is all powerful and useful stuff, and as a species we've created some pretty amazing items, systems and cultures with it.

But, the brain, alone, is a barren place, and being guided solely by the mind can lead you into uncomfortable places with significant dis-ease as a consequence.

In the self-awareness section, we visited the benefits of quietening the mind and learning to rest in awareness as the observer of what is going on.

But what about the heart? Our body doesn't lie. Remember former US president Bill Clinton's assertion: "I did not have sexual relations with that woman!" Do you ever feel uncomfortable, physically, about a decision you've made (or not made); do you find the stresses of daily life show up as tension in the body? Studies have shown that the heart sends more messages to the brain than the other way round, and learning to tune into our body's senses and emotions gives us a much greater steer than over-reliance on the logical mind. Remember that, ultimately, we are driven to accumulate a collection of 'better' feelings. Think about that for a moment: why do you want more money, better relationships, holidays? Because you want to feel better! So it makes sense to tune into how you are feeling and what that is telling you, so you can adjust accordingly.

And what about your soul, spirit or life force (call it what you will), that unmistakable essence of you that somehow feels ethereal, the connection to a bigger purpose, the connection with your own innate sense of self? Do you quieten your mind of whirring thoughts and body of raging emotions long enough to listen to the spirit within you?

We are multi-talented and multi-sensory, receiving and emitting, self-aware and self-repairing organisms that are extraordinarily complicated. Trying to run this organism from the head alone will not lead you down the road to meaningful or authentic success in the long run.

EXERCISE: TAKE TIME OUT, AT LEAST ONCE A WEEK, TO GO FOR A LONG WALK, RUN OR A SIMILAR ACTIVITY, TO RECONNECT WITH YOURSELF AND BRING YOUR HEAD, HEART AND SOUL BACK INTO ALIGNMENT.

JOURNAL ANY INSIGHTS AND NEW INTENTIONS THAT ARISE FROM DOING THIS, AS IT HELPS BRING THEM TO FRUITION LATER.

CHAPTER TWO

CREATING
TRIUMPHS

15. CREATING TRIUMPHS

In the personal mastery section of this book, you will have seen how getting to know yourself better, the authenticity piece, allows you to be less influenced by peers, partners, parents and society at large. You will have seen how, with improved awareness and alignment, you can drive your amazing mind-body-spirit organism much more effectively, and you should have developed constructive attitudes and appreciation. Combined, these skills, insights and ways of being, allow you to be more comfortable in your own skin, grounded and centred in your decision-making, and more effective when interacting with the rest of the world.

When you visited the attachment chapter, you learned that happiness is not 'out there', it is not the pot of gold at the end of the rainbow. You will have learned not to follow the thinking that it will be great when 'such and such' has happened, been bought, achieved, and understood that it's all about the journey not about the destination. So if this is the case, you might well be asking, what is the point of going out there and trying to create success if the work is actually to be totally happy and comfortable with what is?

You could summarize the whole personal mastery section as the journey from 'outside-in' to 'inside-out', which means not looking for success out there to make you feel good inside, although this is the default setting for most of us. Instead, we learn to feel good enough, complete, successful, right here, right now, regardless of external circumstances because in doing so we can show up in day-to-day life with a lightness of touch that is less effortful and more attractive. We are then able to deliver without drama and be more purposeful and productive.

The great irony is that when we are comfortable with ourselves and less needful of the stuff out there, we are able to go out there and achieve far more!

16. THE HARMONY MODEL

PERSONAL		WORK
Health	H	**H**orizon
Activities	A	**A**lignment
Relationships	R	**R**esults
Money	M	**M**odelling
Organised	O	**O**bjectives
Nurture	N	**N**avigate
whys and why nots	Y	**w**hys and why nots

While success is individual to each of us, the following model of mine helps to guide you through the key areas of your personal life and work life. This enables you to make choices that create a harmonious balance between the two, so that you have more purpose, meaning and fulfilment during this one, wild and precious life.

The model is in two halves: on the left-hand side it focuses on your personal life, because if you don't get your personal life in order, it is difficult to be truly effective in the workplace. It covers the four core things that most of us want: enough money, great relationships, to enjoy the activities we do, and good health. But many of us do not achieve these four core things in balance, so we explore the three common reasons we don't manage this, and what we can do about it.

On the business side, whether we are a business owner or employee, we spend a significant amount of lives in the workplace. By using the HARMONY model to look at what you are doing strategically, you can become more effective and fulfilled at work.

17. HEALTH

"IN ORDER FOR MAN TO SUCCEED IN LIFE,
GOD PROVIDED HIM WITH TWO MEANS, EDUCATION AND
PHYSICAL ACTIVITY. NOT SEPARATELY, ONE FOR THE SOUL AND
ONE FOR THE BODY, BUT FOR THE TWO TOGETHER. WITH THESE
TWO MEANS, MAN CAN ATTAIN PERFECTION"
(Plato)

It is very easy to take our health for granted. I know I did. When I lost
my arm following my accident, I was hardly able to walk upstairs. I

was taking 27 prescription tablets a day and I was heavily dependent on the support of others. I gained a first-hand experiential lesson in the importance of being healthy. Without health, everything else becomes far more difficult and hard work. All the major causes of death relate to lifestyle: cancer, cardiac problems, obesity, diabetes and so on, with stress playing a major part too. With good health and fitness, you automatically feel better and everything else becomes easier too.

PHYSICAL EXERCISE

You probably already know that exercise increases levels of feel-good chemicals such as serotonin, norepinephrine and dopamine. However, Dr John J Ratey in his book *Spark!* has scientifically proven that aerobic exercise is far more important than that: "It turns out that moving our muscles produces proteins that travel through the bloodstream and into the brain, where they play pivotal roles in the mechanisms of our highest thought processes."

So what exercise do you do? Are you a couch potato or an extreme sports adrenaline junkie? Or are you somewhere in between? There are two keys to exercise: first, choose an activity you can enjoy, because if you are going to create a habit it had better be an enjoyable one! Second, how do you get out of the door, get the trainers on, or simply just get over the threshold and get started? That's the hard part as the rest follows more easily. My suggestion would be to join a club or a class in the area that interests you, it makes it more sociable, but more importantly, it'll help you maintain the habit.

DIET

"We are what we eat" – lets face it, all the cells in our body are created from what we consume. We all know we should eat at least five portions of fruit and vegetables a day, that we shouldn't eat processed food, that we should maintain a good balance of fats, carbohydrates and proteins. Awareness of the health hazards of sugar is now becoming mainstream, and more and more people are choosing to be gluten- and dairy-free.

I'm not suggesting you become a nutrition freak; in my view, we have kidneys and livers to deal with the toxins in our diet, and like everything else, we use them or lose them. Moreover, excessive worrying about minor flaws in one's diet can lead to the condition known as orthorexia. Like all changes, evolution is often more sustainable than revolution, and particularly with diet when there may be other members of your household who influence what you eat. But what changes can you make? What small new habit could you develop?

EMOTIONAL WELLBEING

We are social animals, we are not designed to do it all ourselves or to work it out alone. What emotional support do you have? Who can you turn to, with whom can you discuss your thoughts, feelings and concerns? Who will be listen to you without judgment, criticism, without trying to fix you? Do you provide the same level of support to anyone else? Do you take part in activities that give back, so you can focus on others rather than yourself? It has been proven that selfless deeds make us feel better.

EXERCISE: IN EACH OF THE THREE CORE AREAS OF HEALTH ABOVE, ASSESS WHERE YOU ARE NOW, AND WHAT YOU WANT TO DO. MAKE A CONSCIOUS CHOICE FOR YOU, NOT WHAT YOU FEEL YOU OUGHT TO DO UNDER DURESS, BUT WHAT YOU REALLY WANT TO DO.

THEN DO IT, LIVE IT, OWN IT.

18. ACTIVITIES

"WE ARE WHAT WE REPEATEDLY DO. EXCELLENCE, THEN, IS NOT AN ACT BUT A HABIT"
(Aristotle)

What activities do you do, at home, at work and for pleasure? When we are consistently doing things we don't like doing, life becomes less enjoyable. So if you are in the wrong job it can have a detrimental effect on everything else. Of course, there are always some things we have to do, which we may prefer not to, but the balance needs to be tipped in your favour. There are also things you may not like doing initially, such as eating healthily or taking regular exercise, which you know will bring rewards further down the line, once you've put in the effort in and set up the habits.

In many ways, our life experience is determined by the decisions we make about how to spend the short time we have on this precious planet. Many of the things we do are seemingly chosen for us by our jobs and life situations (and we have to eat, sleep and ablute!) But we do have choices, and yes, if we want to make significant changes, we may need to disturb the comfort of the present situation, that's an assessment you'll have to make.

Do you find yourself running from pillar-to-post, doing a whole range of activities to suit other people, that you don't particularly enjoy, and in some cases, may not even be particularly good at? If so, how would you prefer it to be? If you had the proverbial magic wand how would you spend your time?

EXERCISE: LIST THE ACTIVITIES YOU DO IN YOUR DAILY LIFE, AND LABEL THEM A,B,C,D AND SO ON.

ON A SCALE OF 1-10, RATE THEM ACCORDING TO HOW MUCH YOU ENJOY DOING THEM, AND HOW GOOD YOU ARE AT THEM.

PLOT THE RESULTS ON THE TABLE BELOW:

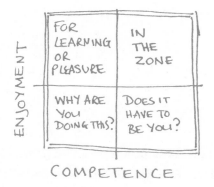

WHAT DO YOU NOTICE?

WHAT CHANGES COULD YOU MAKE?

WHAT CHANGES ARE YOU GOING TO MAKE?

---

19. RELATIONSHIPS

"IF WE COULD CHANGE OURSELVES, THE TENDENCIES IN THE
WORLD WOULD ALSO CHANGE. AS A MAN CHANGES HIS OWN
NATURE, SO DOES THE ATTITUDE OF THE WORLD CHANGE
TOWARDS HIM... WE NEED NOT WAIT TO SEE WHAT OTHERS DO"
(Gandhi)

We have key relationships with people at work, friends and family, our
primary partner if we have one, and, of course, ourselves. When our
relationships are going well, everything else flows more harmoniously.

Conversely, just one toxic relationship can make the world seem a dark place, and when people fall in love, they view the world through rose-tinted spectacles.

BALANCING RELATIONSHIPS AND WORK PRESSURES

The quality of our primary relationship has a profound effect on the rest of our life experience. The demands of the workplace and the pressure to climb the greasy career pole can create challenges that put a strain on primary relationships. But these can enable deeper relationships. (Note for the purposes of simplicity I'm using the archetypal male breadwinner and the female partner with a greater emphasis on home and family – but theses roles and genders can obviously be interchanged.)

A COMMON DYNAMIC

The breadwinner focuses on work because it provides a financial return and is the foundation of providing for the family. His partner can feel there is too much emphasis on work and that he is more interested in work than her. A dynamic ensues where, as he focuses on work, he receives positive validation from his boss and colleagues, which lifts his esteem and status. When he returns home, he anticipates coming into a different environment where he's less accepted and likely to be on the receiving end of the odd small barb or two. So his defences rise even before he's got in the door. His wife, meanwhile, feels uncared for and doesn't receive his full attention. She sees him being far more interested in work than his family, and doesn't buy his story about providing financial support. She knows it's more than that; he prefers to spend time at work than time with her – and that hurts. The dynamic gently polarizes and intensifies over time: the less cared for she feels, the pickier she becomes to gain his attention. The pickier she becomes, the less he likes it, and so he continues to focus his attention at work where the rewards are clearer.

However, it doesn't have to be this way, there are things you can do to shift the patterns radically, change the dynamic and breathe new life into the relationship.

1. Recognize and accept this dynamic

Just recognizing and accepting this dynamic, or your particular variant of it, can create a profound shift in perspective. Do this without blame, criticism or judgment. Just see if you can both agree what is actually going on, without any attempt to fix it at this stage. This is an important step – don't rush into solution mode! It takes two to tango, so the blame game is unhelpful and always ends in an attack-and-defend dynamic and trench warfare – don't go there, there will be no winners. Simply accept where you are, and see if you can find a common willingness to create a better dynamic.

2. Communication is key

Sadly, communication is often one of the first casualties of a relationship going off the boil. A common pattern is the princess's belief that "if my knight in shining armour really loved me, he'd know what my needs were and would fulfil them without me having to ask". Alas, this is a train crash waiting to happen – your knight in shining armour is too busy attending to his own battles, and despite all his skills, he is not a mind reader. Also, are you really clear what your own needs actually are? How about expressing some of those needs clearly, specifically and without code, and request (not demand) that he might like to help you fulfil those needs? On the surface, it seems less romantic, but upon reflection, it is pretty romantic to think that you could ask your shining knight what you'd like, and enjoy the pleasure of him delivering on your wishes? It has to be better than trench warfare, surely? You can start with really simple things that have a higher chance of success; for example, "could you put out the bins on Thursday night?"

3. The five love languages

If you've recognized and accepted the dynamic you've co-created and opened up clearer communication, you are already making great strides towards repairing the relationship. However, sometimes we communicate our love in different ways and this can lead to love being lost in translation. Gary Chapman's book *The Five Love Languages* suggests: words of affirmation, quality time, receiving gifts, acts of service and physical touch are the five different languages of love. The trick is to determine the languages that are important to your partner and make a commitment to communicate more in the language they prefer.

While everyone's profile is different, a very common dynamic is that the man prefers words of affirmation and physical touch, while the woman prefers quality time and acts of service. The exact opposite to receiving words of affirmation is to be on the receiving end of pickiness, micro-jabs and 'the look' – these things can become disproportionately corrosive for a man.

The common truism around physical touch is that a man seeks intimacy through sex while a woman wants to establish intimacy before considering sex. A seemingly deadlocked dynamic! This is where quality time with non-sexual touch is so important, whether it's holding hands while going for a walk, or gently stroking her hair when watching a DVD one evening, quality time and physical touch can both be achieved without sex being on the agenda. Try it out and see what happens!

Accepting the relationship dynamic without blame and judgment, opening up clearer communication and communicating in the other person's love languages, can make wholesale improvements in the relationship, and for many couples, this can be enough to get them back on track. Ultimately, however, to have a truly fulfilling relationship, it helps if both partners are fully comfortable with themselves so they are not looking for the partner to make them 'whole'. This is where the personal mastery section is so valuable.

EXERCISE

WHERE ARE YOU WITH YOUR PRIMARY RELATIONSHIPS RIGHT NOW?

COULD THINGS BE BETTER?

WHAT CAN YOU DO ABOUT THE WAY YOU SHOW UP IN THOSE RELATIONSHIPS? (REMEMBER, WE CAN'T CHANGE ANYONE ELSE)

20. MONEY

**"MONEY, MONEY, MONEY – MUST BE FUNNY,
IN A RICH MAN'S WORLD"
(ABBA)**

Money is like oxygen, if you don't have enough of it, it can be hard to breathe and uncomfortable. But how much is enough? Could you get by with less? And, as with oxygen, having masses to spare doesn't actually make that much difference. There is no shortage of unhappy – very financially wealthy – people, often living in splendid isolation. In many ways, our life experience is determined by the decisions we make about how to spend the short time we have on this precious planet. Money can offer us more choice about how we spend our time, and thereby allow us to have a richer life experience. But the trick is to ensure money remains the slave and does not become the master. What is the point of being focused on material wealth, to the detriment of your health, activities and relationships?

Money is an exchange medium, it is a form of potential energy. So it's what you do with it and how you keep it flowing that really matters. The way in which we relate to money usually falls into one of the sacred money archetypes. With which do you feel most naturally aligned?

The eight archetypes are:

1. The Ruler – creates an empire, but can never relax
2. The Maverick – takes risks, but can lose it all
3. The Accumulator – handles money and finances wisely, but can be mean-spirited
4. The Celebrity – high profile leader, but can spend to avoid feeling empty
5. The Alchemist – creates ideas and possibilities, but can fail to capitalize on them
6. The Connector – a natural networker, but doesn't feel empowered by money
7. The Romantic – believes there is always more, but may overspend in the meantime
8. The Nurturer – provides amazing value, but may forget about self

It's worth Googling for an assessment if you are not sure of your tendencies.

That said, Mr Micawber's famous, and oft-quoted, recipe for happiness remains relevant:

> **"ANNUAL INCOME TWENTY POUNDS,**
> **ANNUAL EXPENDITURE NINETEEN [POUNDS] NINETEEN**
> **[SHILLINGS] AND SIX [PENCE], RESULT HAPPINESS. ANNUAL**
> **INCOME TWENTY POUNDS, ANNUAL EXPENDITURE TWENTY**
> **POUNDS OUGHT AND SIX, RESULT MISERY"**
> (**Charles Dickens,** *David Copperfield*)

EXERCISE: REFLECT – IS MONEY YOUR MASTER OR YOUR SLAVE?

HOW COULD YOU REDUCE YOUR EXPENDITURE WITHOUT MAKING A SIGNIFICANT DIFFERENCE TO YOUR EXPERIENCES (A POSH COFFEE A DAY COULD SET YOU BACK £1,000 A YEAR – AFTER TAX!)

HOW COULD YOU INCREASE YOUR INCOME? WOULD THE SACRIFICES BE WORTH IT, OR IS IT A QUESTION OF SETTING YOUR MIND TO IT?

COULD YOU, OR DO YOU, SAVE 10% OF YOUR INCOME?

21. ORGANIZED

Let's face it, if you asked almost anyone in the street whether they'd like good health, to enjoy the activities they do, to have great relationships and enough money, they'd say "yes". And yet relatively few of us manage to achieve this consistently. This is where the ONY part of the HARMONY model comes in:

All four areas of health, activities, relationships and money are interrelated. When we are stressed about money, for example, it can affect our relationships negatively, adding to our stress, which impacts our health negatively, which then impacts on the way we show up in the activities we do. That is why it's so important to get these four areas working well, in balance and in tune with one another.

One of the reasons this doesn't routinely happen is because it doesn't happen by accident, you need to make conscious choices about each of these areas in your life and then do something about them. That means getting organized, taking time out to review and reflect, and continuing to do this periodically as needs and life situations change over the years.

The conventional way to get organized is to map out your five-year goals, work backwards systematically, and cut the stages down into smaller steps. If you're the kind of person for whom this works, you're probably doing it already and I take my hat off to you. Personally, I've never managed to make that system work for me, so my take on it goes like this:

Pick the one area of your life in which you can make the easiest impact, and focus on doing that. You will find that, as you experience the improvement in that area, it will make you feel uplifted and give you more enthusiasm to address the next thing. Pick the simplest thing, which gives you an easy win, so that you do not fall into the trap of working on your biggest weakness, which typically leads to little progress, subsequent discouragement and retreating into making no improvements whatsoever.

EXERCISE: WHAT IS YOUR PREFERRED WAY
OF BECOMING ORGANIZED?

DOES IT WORK FOR YOU?

IF NOT HOW COULD YOU ADAPT IT?

SO WHAT ARE YOU GOING TO DO NOW?

22. NURTURE

It's all too easy to get caught up in the pursuit of perfection and to be influenced by the stereotypical media images of successful people to which we are meant to live up. We convince ourselves we are not good enough, and mercilessly give ourselves a hard time. Have you ever noticed how you talk to yourself? When you make a mistake does your inner critic berate you in a tone, and with a choice of words, you'd never use with anyone else? If so, you are not alone, I used to do it as a matter of course, and most people I know take a similar approach.

The problem is, we cannot beat ourselves into greatness; it simply isn't an effective strategy. One of the advantages of doing the mindfulness work in the personal mastery section is that it becomes easier to become aware of the language and tone of your inner critic. Simply noticing is a good first step; over time, replace the harsh words with more accepting and supportive communication. You need to develop your inner critic into your best, most supportive friend, one who knows you are being the best you can be, who knows you are human and make mistakes. Learning to live, love and truly accept ourselves as we are is, paradoxically, the key to moving forwards. When we do so, we tame the inner critic, create less internal resistance and thereby learn to get out of our own way and be more effective.

Learn to tame your inner critic into being your supportive friend. In mastering this, you'll find you are more adept at guiding yourself back on track when your inner chimp wants to be distracted by short-term rewards rather than long-term gains. (*The Chimp Paradox* – Steve Peters)

Remember, none of us has a complete toolkit, a full set of skills and abilities, so seek out and ask for support in the areas in which you need it. It is your own responsibility to do so.

EXERCISE: HOW HARSH IS YOUR INNER CRITIC?

REVISIT THE MINDFULNESS SECTION

DEVELOP A MORE SUPPORTIVE APPROACH TO LOOKING AFTER YOURSELF

23. WHY?/
WHY NOT? – PERSONAL

(Phonetically it's a Y!)

It's all well and good setting out positive intentions about what you want to BE, DO and HAVE, so that you have plenty of time, money, relationships, enjoy the activities you do and are in rude health. But it can be like setting New Year's resolutions; the gym membership is taken out with full enthusiasm and a determination to be the envisaged fitter, slimmer version of yourself, yet after a few weeks, normal patterns of behaviour creep back in, only this time you have the added disappointment of perceived failure.

To help overcome these challenges so that failure doesn't become inevitable, it helps to link the challenge to a higher purpose, goal or reason. This will make it easier to work through your resistance. In other words, what's your 'why'? Or as Simon Sinek (author of *Start With Why*) would have us do, start with your 'why'. Being clear about your 'why', provides the guidance and motivation when distractions occur along the way.

One of the biggest challenges is being comfortable, and there are two challenges here. When we are comfortable it can be difficult to motivate ourselves to move to a better place. It can be even more challenging when we grow comfortable with the familiar, because it seems safe to primitive parts of our brains, which means that even when dysfunctional procrastinating behaviour becomes the norm, it feels familiar and comfortable and is difficult to overcome.

Alongside your 'why', what are your 'why nots'? What's stopping you? What are your blocks?

When you focus the torchlight of awareness on your personal blocks, they can start to ease and lift a little; sometimes, however, it is useful to work with a coach to help release them and create new, more empowering, habits.

On a practical level, getting started on a new activity can be the hardest part, so, for example, when running, the toughest thing can be putting on your training shoes and getting out of the door. Try putting out your running kit beforehand so it's ready and waiting for you!

EXERCISE: FOR EACH CHANGE YOU SEEK, WHAT IS YOUR GUIDING 'WHY'?

WHAT ARE THE LIKELY RESISTANCES THAT YOU WILL CREATE AS YOU SEEK TO MAKE THOSE CHANGES?

WHAT CAN YOU DO TO LOOSEN THE GRIP OF THOSE RESISTANCES?

24. WHY? WHY/NOT? – IN THE WORKPLACE

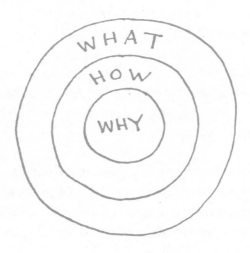

In his book and TED talk, Simon Sinek describes how to start with 'why' and explains his golden circles. He explains that starting with 'why' engages you with the limbic system part of the brain, the part that governs emotion and behaviour, where our 'gut feelings' arise. When you engage with this part of the brain, the rational part of the brain, the neocortex, will take on board the data of 'how and what' with much more interest. Typically, people and organizations start the other way round, starting with 'what', then explaining the 'how' and the 'why'. The problem with this approach is that, straight away, the rational neocortex finds all the reasons to be uninterested in what is being said.

Why are you working? Probably just to make money... but why this workplace, why this line of work? Did you arrive here deliberately or was it a succession of seemingly random events? Was it because you wanted to be here or was it what your parents wanted for you, for example?

Why did you not choose the alternative paths open to you?

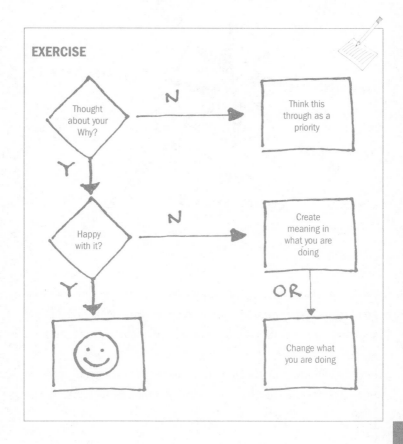

EXERCISE

25. NAVIGATE

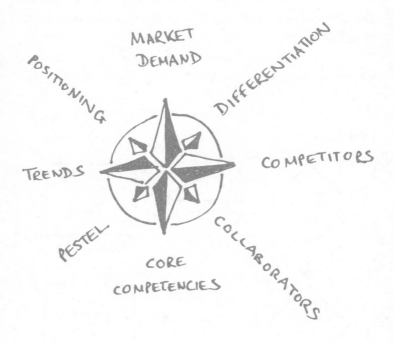

Whether you are running your own business or progressing your own career in the corporate world, having a strategic understanding of the world around you allows you to navigate with more skill and insight.

The diagram above offers areas to consider as you match your own personal strengths (core competencies, in management speak) with market demand for what you offer.

On the left-hand side, PESTEL is shorthand for political, economic, social, technical, environment and legal factors or changes that may be occurring in the wider context of where you are working. Some, or all, of these may be affecting trends in your marketplace. On the right-hand side of the diagram, you are asked to consider your allies and foes along the way. By considering these factors, you can work out how to create a position in the minds of the people that matter (your customers or bosses) that is valuable and sets you apart in a good way (differentiates) from everyone else.

EXERCISE: WORK THROUGH THIS DIAGRAM
FOR YOURSELF.

WHAT INSIGHTS HAVE YOU GAINED?

WHAT ARE YOU GOING TO DO DIFFERENTLY NOW?

26. OBJECTIVES

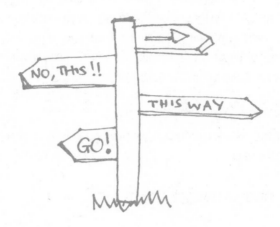

**"IF YOU DON'T KNOW WHERE YOU'RE GOING,
ANY ROAD WILL GET YOU THERE"**
(often quoted as being in *Alice in Wonderland* –
though that is never actually said there!)

The clearer the target, the easier it is to reach it. The challenge is that
there are often too many objectives, which can create confusion and
a fear of missing out on other potentially interesting projects that may
distract you along the way – shiny object syndrome!

The trick is to have as few objectives as possible and to keep them simple. That way, they are easy to communicate and keep consistent.

For example, when we built 4Networking (a national network of business breakfast networking meetings), the top-level objective was "to create a national network" – that was it, clear and simple. It gave direction and focus without being constrained by timescales and detail. The message remained the same from the business inception until the national network was completed over the course of five years. (Then international expansion started!)

The secondary levels change over time, as needs change, and the third-tier-objectives are where the details and day-to-day requirements are required. But when these all link up to supporting the one, or few, very clear and consistent objectives at the top, the results can be stunning.

EXERCISE: IF YOU HAD TO CUT DOWN ALL YOUR OBJECTIVES TO SELECT ONE OVERRIDING FOCUS, WHAT WOULD IT BE?

IS IT SUFFICIENTLY CLEAR, SIMPLE AND CONSISTENT TO CHART YOUR JOURNEY FOR THE NEXT FEW YEARS?

27. MODELLING

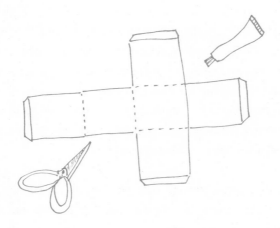

We live in a complex world that is always changing, and we are changing within it. Modelling allows us to make sense of complex situations by simplifying and structuring things in a logical way. While models are extremely useful, remember the model is just a representation or map – and the map is not the territory.

A quick dictionary search of the word 'model' brings up different definitions, according to use:

NOUN: A standard or example for imitation or comparison

ADJECTIVE: Worthy to serve as a model; example: a model student

VERB: To form or plan according to a model

So how does modelling show up in your life?

Do you wish to emulate anyone in particular, is there someone who inspires you? Try to model some of their behaviours.

Have you mastered a particular set of skills or behaviours that could act as a model for others to follow or emulate?

Have you used the models in this book, and elsewhere, to help you plan your way forward in life and at work?

In the workplace, business models of different types crop up everywhere. When I took my MBA, I was taught about the dangers of organizations separating into different departments that follow their own agendas, losing sight of the overall vision, and failing to cooperate with other departments. These are known as functional silos. The irony is that they taught the course in functional silos too! So I developed my own model to simplify the whole business model picture in a way that is aligned, appropriate, affordable and actionable.

It shows the four core areas of any business: sales and marketing, operations, people, finance – overlapping. All are focused on serving the customer's needs efficiently, effectively and profitably.

The key with overlapping is that when thinking and modelling in your life and your workplace, there is a series of 'both-ands' to consider: social and technical, customer and suppliers, profit and purpose, hard skills and soft skills, strategy and tactics, inputs and outputs, ebbs and flows,

Of course, it makes it harder to focus on the polar opposites and make them both right and effective, but that is where the juice is, that is where the work is, and that is where you can make the difference.

EXERCISE: DO THE WORK IN THIS HARMONY MODEL FOR YOUR PERSONAL LIFE AND WORK LIFE.

WHERE ARE YOU JUST FOCUSING ON ONE SIDE OF THE COIN, AND NOT WORKING WITH BOTH SIDES?

28. RESULTS

We all want results, and we want them fast. We live in a quick-win society, the quick fix, the life hack, the want it all, want it now culture.

However, in reality, results come through persistent, well-managed actions.

There are three things that are really important when considering results. Results need to be as close to 'real time' as possible; they must focus as much on inputs as outputs; and the results must be clear. That way, any feedback can be used to adjust behaviour and change the outcome positively.

REAL TIME

Many business owners wait for the accountant's profit and loss figures to gauge how well their business is doing. The problem with this is that the information is often very late (at best, weeks behind), focuses on outputs, and is obscured with amortization, depreciation and other accounting adjustments. While good accounting information is essential for financial decision-making, it is not great for day-to-day operational performance. And it is operational performance that is the prime input towards the output of financial performance. So, in your own workplace, how can you gain quicker operational information?

INPUTS AS WELL AS OUTPUTS

The key question is "what are the activities that drive performance?" If you want to lose weight, for example, there is little point in weighing yourself every day because measuring the output doesn't change anything. You also need to measure the inputs, in this case, food intake and exercise. To a large extent, if you take care of the inputs the outputs take care of themselves.

In your workplace, what are the activities that drive performance? What are the inputs that matter?

CLARITY

We live in an information age, with our phones and watches able to track seemingly everything. The problem is information overload. Focus on the few important areas that have the most impact, and create a way of measuring these clearly and simply.

For example, in a car, the dashboard displays the real time results of the car as it is being driven.

EXERCISE: WHAT ARE THE IMPORTANT INPUTS
AND OUTPUTS IN YOUR LIFE AND WORK?

HOW COULD YOU CREATE YOUR OWN DASHBOARD TO KEEP
TRACK OF PROGRESS?

29. ALIGNMENT

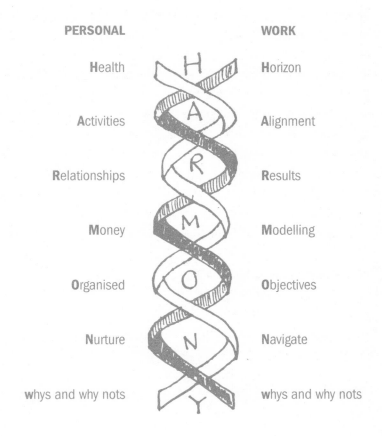

PERSONAL		WORK
Health	H	**H**orizon
Activities	A	**A**lignment
Relationships	R	**R**esults
Money	M	**M**odelling
Organised	O	**O**bjectives
Nurture	N	**N**avigate
whys and why nots	Y	**w**hys and why nots

The purpose of modelling is to simplify and structure complicated things. Life is complex, and even in the simplified HARMONY model, which covers personal life and work life, there are plenty of sub-models and exercises.

It is important to align these as best you can. Keeping with the car analogy, if your wheels are not aligned, steering becomes difficult and tyre wear is much greater. Ultimately, if things get too far out of alignment, wheels start to fall off!

Alignment is when you start bringing everything together: the self-leadership through personal mastery, the strategic leadership through standing back from the coal face and considering what is going on and where to go next, and from that space, working with others to bring out the best in them to align what you are trying to achieve with what they are trying to achieve.

EXERCISE: REVISIT THE WORK YOU'VE DONE WITH
THE DIFFERENT SECTIONS OF THE HARMONY MODEL.

DO THEY WORK WELL TOGETHER?
IS THERE TOO MUCH TO DO?

WHAT COULD YOU DISCARD OR LET GO OF?

HOW COULD YOU MAKE IT MORE ACHIEVABLE AND LESS
STRESSFUL?

30. HORIZON

**"IF YOU DON'T HAVE A DREAM, HOW YOU GONNA
HAVE A DREAM COME TRUE?"**
(Oscar Hammerstein II)

Much of this book deals with the practical issues many of us face. But
while it's important and useful to follow these strategies for success,
it is also vital to ask yourself where they are leading.

Do you have a dream? In my experience, by the time formal education and the workplace have moulded us over the years, most people have lost touch with their dreams and settled for a consumerist hamster-wheel existence, which they've been conditioned to endure.

However, if you do have a dream, what are you doing to make it come true? Have you written it down, communicated it to others, taken the first steps, made plans and got underway? Or not? What's stopping you? What have you got to lose?

If you don't have a dream, and find yourself caught up in the routine of life with all the demands it places upon you, how would you like it to be different? It doesn't have to be some grand world-changing plan or scheme, but simply a new vision for how you'd like your life to be as you proceed through the years.

The key here is to remember that you do have a choice about how you respond to life and its events. You have a choice about how you imagine your future and the reasons behind that. And you have the option of taking personal responsibility for doing something about it – or not. The choice is indeed yours.

"IMAGINATION IS MORE IMPORTANT THAN KNOWLEDGE. FOR KNOWLEDGE IS LIMITED TO ALL WE NOW KNOW AND UNDERSTAND, WHILE IMAGINATION EMBRACES THE ENTIRE WORLD, AND ALL THERE EVER WILL BE TO KNOW AND UNDERSTAND"
(Albert Einstein)

Just being reminded of the above can be helpful sometimes, because it distils and simplifies things. It reminds us that we have more choices than we sometimes let ourselves believe when we take the 'easy' option of allowing life to happen to us, rather than setting out to create the life we want to lead.

EXERCISE: DARE TO DREAM.

DREAM OFTEN, NURTURE THE IDEAS THAT REPEAT
OR BECOME ENGAGING.

THEN DO SOMETHING ABOUT IT!

CHAPTER THREE

DEALING WITH DISASTER

31. DEALING WITH DISASTER

I've been fortunate enough to have experienced significant success in my life: two multi-million pound businesses, a long marriage, three great children, private education, lovely holidays, houses, cars, world travel, sporting achievements and so on. But the journey has come with its fair share of setbacks along the way, from the common academic/job interview setbacks in my twenties, to redundancy, negative equity and coping with debt. I've also had to deal with negotiating forced exits from both my businesses, and recovering from a serious car accident where I lost my arm. Finally, going through a divorce after 26 years with my wife, gave me the time on my own to research and reflect on my journey and write this book.

One of the things I've learned is that dealing with disaster is the flipside of creating success. They are different sides of the same coin. And as Rudyard Kipling reminds us in his poem *"IF"* :

IF you can meet with Triumph and Disaster
And treat those two imposters just the same.....
Yours is the earth and everything that's in it

What I think he means is that we inevitably go through ups and downs in life, and let's face it, it would be boring if it didn't have this contrast. But rather than clinging on to the 'successes' and shying away from the 'disasters', we should embrace it all, it's all going to happen – so take it on as breadth of experience in all its richness.

You may be thinking, "yeah right, who are you trying to kid? Give me the good times all the way!", but let me tell you this: the journey since losing my arm has more than made up for its loss. Sure, I didn't plan to have that setback in my life, and parts of the journey have been unbelievably painful, physically, emotionally and mentally. The bottom line is we plan for success but disasters happen, it's a fact of life. These disasters help shape us and help us to grow our abilities, capabilities and compassion. As we develop our resilience, we are able to embrace more and be less fearful of what might be, because we know that, one way or another, we'll be able to handle it, and that's an empowering place to be.

This section of the book leads you through strategies and insights to help you work through the hard times.

32. DEALING WITH FEAR

When we hit hard times, the biggest overall challenge is dealing with fear. Our response to fear is driven by our primitive instinctive brain mechanism that generates the fight/flight/freeze response and the body is flooded with cortisol and adrenaline. This is great when the danger is a short-term one such as coming across a lion out on the savannah, and where natural physical activity dissipates the build up of chemicals secreted in the blood. The problem is that, in our modern-day existence, the perceived threats are rarely immediately life-threatening, but still invoke the same chemical response. Worse still, because many of the problems are situational, rather than isolated events, it is common to remain in this fearful state for extended periods. In society, we rename this condition stress – and there's almost a pandemic of it.

When we feel stressed, our decision-making is more influenced by our primitive brain, with knee-jerk, black-and-white thinking. It is less influenced by the nuanced emotional decision-making of the limbic system and the creative thought process of the neocortex part of the brain.

Recognizing this fundamental mechanism at play is really helpful when using the other strategies suggested in this book. Each of the strategies is, in its own separate way, trying to help you see a way forward, despite the challenges of the present and the uncertainties of the future.

When we are stressed, being told "just relax" seems nonsensical; how can you relax when there is this threat to attend to? However, we are much more effective at dealing with threats when we are relaxed, and better able to access the more evolved parts of our brain. What this means is that it's useful to have ways of reframing the situation, to make it easier to get to a relaxed state so you can become effective again.

The two core anchors of your stress response toolkit are breathing and exercise.

BREATH

We breathe all the time, consciously or not. When we are stressed, we get wrapped up in our heads and our breathing becomes shallow and tight. Taking a few moments to close your eyes and to breathe deeply from your lower abdomen, helps you escape the whirring thoughts in your mind and reach the calm, stable feeling that is always available to us when we breathe deeply. Taking a few deep breaths several times a day is a habit well worth cultivating. Gently stroking your forehead or cheeks at the same time also helps ease stress.

EXERCISE

Regular aerobic exercise helps dissipate the cortisol that is stored in the body when we feel stressed and releases endorphins and other feel-good chemicals in your body. So it's a double whammy: you get to dump a bunch of bad chemicals and gain a bunch of good ones. And, of course, when you are fitter and healthier, you feel better and more able to deal with the challenges that you face. At the two very bleakest moments of my life, placing significant extra emphasis on physical exercise proved to be the singlemost effective strategy helping me to move through the difficult ongoing situations.

YOUR EXERCISE: GET OUT AND GET FIT

RETURN TO CONSCIOUS BREATHING AT LEAST SIX TIMES A DAY.

33. DITCH SMART GOALS

At times of distress, SMART (specific, measurable, achievable, realistic and time-bound) goals don't work. SMART goals work well in a logical planning scenario, when you know what you're doing and have the relevant resources to hand. Essentially, SMART goals are a way of being managed and being accountable to someone. When it feels as if your world has fallen apart, it's all too much, goals seem unachievable, planning is fruitless because you know you are going to fail. You already feel overburdened and overwhelmed, so adding this on top will feel like a recipe for disaster.

So what can you do? In my experience, setting a compass point and committing to baby steps in that direction, is hugely effective. The compass gives you direction, it's clear and simple, it doesn't matter how lost you appear to be, how many wrong turns you may have made, the compass point is always there to give you the same consistent direction. By taking baby steps, it shifts your focus from outputs, to inputs, it's easier to achieve something, and therefore start to feel a little better about yourself. When you start to feel a little better about yourself, you reduce the stress and are then more able to access the more evolved parts of your brain.

Conversely, when you stick to a SMART-goal programme within a defined planning framework (which works well when you are working well!) you end up making yourself feel worse, more stressed and frightened. With a SMART-goal programme, you gain more and more evidence of how badly you are performing, and the cycle of despair is intensified. With a compass point and baby steps, you can have down days, distraction days and downright duvet days, and still be able to check in with your compass, take more baby steps and take comfort in small achievements.

Relentless small steps in a single direction achieve great results, often taking you further than originally planned at the outset. But when there is no single direction set, you will not reach the required result. When Winnie-the-Pooh set out in a snowstorm in the hundred-acre wood, he travelled many, many paces, but always landed out where he started, because he had no direction.

As an example, after returning from hospital following my car accident, I was so physically weak that it took me a whole five minutes to get myself up a single flight of stairs. At the top of the staircase I was so shocked that, in that instant, I vowed to get fit. That was it: no specifics, no 'how tos', no targets, no timescales, just a single compass-point direction, that was it. Clear, simple and unambiguous. By taking baby steps such as reaching the letterbox at the end of the road and back and so on, I eventually moved further and faster. Rehabilitation in the hydrotherapy pool introduced swimming to me. Later on, somehow, a bicycle was introduced, and a couple of years later I was competing in an Olympic-distance triathlon! An achievement that was far bigger than I would have believed possible at the outset. I am certain that if I had set that goal at the start, it would have demotivated me. It would have seemed impossibly difficult, and I would have felt dispirited along the way because I had allowed my focus to be on the destination (the output) rather the journey (the input).

EXERCISE: HOW CAN YOU SIMPLIFY YOUR LIFE BY CHOOSING ONE, TWO OR THREE (NO MORE) CLEAR COMPASS-POINT DIRECTIONS TOWARDS WHICH YOU CAN TAKE CONSISTENT BABY STEPS?

34. DO THE WORK

Revisit the personal mastery section of this book

AUTHENTICITY

What's true for you right now? What would you do if you had the freedom to do what you wanted? Could you do that?

ATTITUDE

When things aren't going well it's easy to get down in the dumps, it's through conscious choice that we choose what we focus on. You can choose to wallow in self-pity, or you can choose to reframe the situation to a more positive one. Typically, when we are down, we frame problems as being pervasive, persistent and personal. By pervasive, we mean that it's happening everywhere, so if one thing goes wrong, we think that everything has gone wrong. By persistent we mean that because it's bad now it will always be bad. And by personal, we mean that everything that's bad that's happening is personally directed at us. When we think this way, it makes matters worse, far worse. It becomes a self-fulfilling prophecy, so at least we can have the dumb self-satisfaction of being right!

When we learn, or remember, to reframe these problems as specific, short term and 'shit happens!', life becomes more manageable. By specific, we mean that if something is going wrong in one area of your life, it doesn't mean it applies everywhere else. By short term, it reminds us that "this too will pass", no feeling is permanent. Even when permanent things happen (like losing my arm, for example) over time you learn to adapt and (like me), you might even become grateful for the journey on which this experience has taken you. By remembering that 'shit happens', it depersonalizes it; it's part of life, sometimes it's easy, sometimes it's hard, get over it!

AWARENESS

Remember to take time to still the mind, to notice how your thoughts influence your feelings and lock you into habitual patterns of behaviour. The more you become aware of how you create dramas, for example, to avoid facing your own fears and take the self-responsibility to do something about them, the easier it is to alter your approach. If nothing else, taking time out to breathe and still the mind will help.

ACCEPTANCE

Are you resisting what's going on right now? Should life not be like this? Is it unfair? What you resist persists. Through accepting 'what is' as 'it is' – it is what it is – you are able to free up the wasted energy spent wishing things were different and use it in more constructive ways.

APPRECIATION

What we appreciate appreciates. Both practically and metaphorically, when we appreciate something we increase its value to ourselves in an upward spiralling cycle. What we focus on, we tend to get more of, so when we focus on the bad stuff, we tend to see more of it and attract more of it. When we focus on the good stuff, we tend to see more of it and attract more of it. When we consciously choose to appreciate what we already have, it makes us feel better, and feeling better is the key to being more effective in life.

ATTACHMENT

Letting go of the things, people and dreams that we have cherished can be excruciatingly difficult. Learning to let go of what has gone, and to focus on the present, with a hopeful view of the future, will help you enjoy your life more easefully. Care deeply without attachment to the outcome, focus on the inputs and less on the outputs, experience the journey rather than fretting about the destination. It's all the same gig when you boil it down.

ALIGNMENT

Do you feel like you are being pulled from pillar-to-post, as the expression goes? Whose agenda are you following? Are you trying to do too much? What would happen if you didn't have to be superman or superwoman? What if you could give yourself a break and focus on the few things that are truly important to you and let the rest find its own way, so that your head, heart and soul could be as one, and you could ride life's journey more in flow?

35. ABC VOIDING

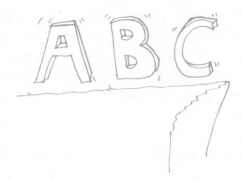

A-VOIDING

Have you noticed that we live in a distraction society? We are bombarded with advertisements to encourage us to want more, to do more, to experience more. We have media bombarding us with disaster and blame stories to make us feel powerless, and consequently, many of us distract ourselves, lest we meet up with ourselves, or turn to drink or drugs to dull the pain.

But what is it we are avoiding? What would be so terrifying if we stopped for a while, stepped off the hamster wheel to just 'be' with ourselves, let our thoughts and feelings come and go, without fear or judgment, and discerned our own sense from that place or space?

B-VOIDING

After my car accident, in hospital, I had a near death experience. I didn't watch my life flash in front of me, nor did I see a tunnel of light or go to some wondrous place. For me, it was an experience of total darkness, total silence, total peace; a release of all fears, concerns and responsibilities, a total freedom, if you will. At the time, I didn't see the significance of this experience because it didn't match the perceived norm, and I was focusing on rebuilding my life. But now, I recognize this as a place to which I can consciously return, a place of stillness and letting go, it's like pressing the reset button, just by being in the void (B-Void), and resting there.

C-VOIDING

When we are wrapped up in the day's events and stresses and dramas take over, it's not easy to switch gear. In these instances, it's tricky to have a more empowered, positive and relaxed perspective on life. This is why it's so easy to get caught up in the avoidance loop – A-void – staying away from the void, the emptiness, the nothingness, that's what all the distraction is about. But when you turn, face and embrace the void, rest and be with it, it's like shifting out of gear and into neutral. From that neutral place, it's much easier to see more clearly (C-void) and from there move into a gear of your choice.

EXERCISE: I DARE YOU TO TAKE TIME OUT TO BE WITH YOURSELF, TO MEET YOURSELF IN THE VAST EXPANSE OF NOTHINGNESS IN WHICH WE EXIST, AND SEE WHAT HAPPENS.

36. TIMING

Timing has such a strong bearing on life and yet we are conditioned, in many ways, to ignore the natural cycles. The backdrop of our culture is one of relentless progress and growth in GDP. A linear progression, if you will; things are permanently getting better. But that is an illusion, and this illusion makes us feel worse when things are not going better. When we recognize that things ebb and flow like the tides, it is easier to accept the rough and the smooth of life's journey. Accepting this allows the rich tapestry of life to be appreciated rather than resisted.

All living things are born from a seed and grow and develop, decay and decline. When we are young, we have different aspirations to when we reach our middle and older ages. In fact, one of the more exciting things about the current time is that there are many more phases to life than the young, middle and old ages of the past.

As we live longer and are healthier, we have more options. Not so long ago, the perceived norm was to grow up (youth), get a job, build a nest to house a family (middle age), carry on working till retirement (old age) and die. Now people have families much later, so have a new chapter in their 20s and 30s, and when the children have flown the nest in our 50s or 60s, we still have the health and vitality to begin another new chapter. Where people would die a few years after retirement at 65 (which was what the national insurance pension calculations used to be based on!) now many people are healthy and active well into their 80s and beyond, for some.

This has radical implications, because if you find yourself in a difficult place, it is very easy to slip into the thinking that you'll be stuck there, but this is very rarely the case. Things change, things happen, we change our perspectives and our understanding develops (if we allow this to happen). The magical thing is that when we recognize and embrace these changes, it becomes easier to move through change.

In fact, learning to accept, embrace and enjoy change is a cornerstone of a happy life. It means that when you are with someone, you recognize you'll never be with them just like this again, because the next time (and, of course, we don't know what is around the corner, so there may never be a next time) they will be a different person. They will have changed, and so will you. What this means is that each meeting is new, however slight the changes might be. When we are sufficiently open to the fact that each encounter is new, rather than working from our pigeonholed short-hand assumptions of the past, life takes on a whole new vibrancy – and that is worth waking up for!

In business, timing is everything. There is an economic backdrop of the boom/bust, greed-based growth and recessionary correction cycles that relentlessly repeat themselves. There is the market acceptance of a new product or idea – no-one would set up a business selling fax machines now, but in the late 1980s it was a booming market. And there is the cycle of the business itself as it transitions from start-up through growth and plateaus. This provides choice points along the way, either to stay stuck on the plateau, decline and wither on the vine, or to choose conscious growth. Whenever we are stuck in our journey, we have the same three choices. We can ignore the symptoms and carry on being stuck, hit total despair and give up and spiral downwards to a disengaged way of being, or recognize the challenges and choose to work through them. However long and uncertain the journey ahead may be, it's your call. What are you going to choose?

EXERCISE: WHAT ASPECTS OF YOUR LIFE CAN YOU VIEW THROUGH THE LENS OF TIMING CYCLES?

HOW DOES THAT CHANGE YOUR PERSPECTIVE ON WHAT'S GOING ON?

HOW WILL YOU APPROACH THINGS MORE EASEFULLY AND GRACEFULLY AS A RESULT OF THIS INSIGHT?

37. TOWING

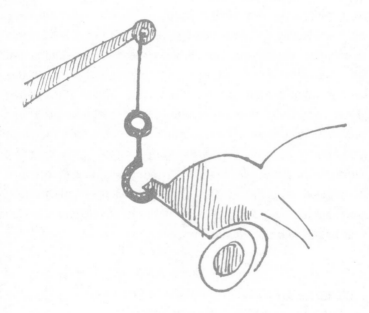

We can't do it all on our own, we form families, communities, organizations and societies precisely because we are social animals with different skill sets and personalities. Together, we can achieve far more, and together is intrinsically more enjoyable than being alone (assuming you have some personal space, of course!). In fact, one of my hallmark sayings is "one-man bands don't work" (first announced in public to an audience of 100 one-man bands – but that's another story).

The challenge is that, when we are feeling low, it can be difficult to ask for help, as we feel we'll be a burden on others. Yet, when we ask people for support, it can drift into an offloading of woes and difficulties, and that only goes to strengthen the neural pathways in the brain concerned with challenges, so you feel worse. Friends grow tired of the same stories being repeated over and over, and in time, drift away.

But at the times in life when I've been most challenged, people have appeared to lend support, from practical help in the form of making meals or mowing the lawn, to providing help and encouragement with fitness training, or uplifting personal relationships. The trick is to accept and embrace support. People like to be valued, appreciated and to be of service. Honour that by receiving the support whole-heartedly and working with them to move forward in some way.

It doesn't matter that they are not fixing everything, it matters that you now know you are not alone and that you are making some progress in some areas of your life. Work with whatever is working, work with what is easiest to fix. This is the opposite of working with your weaknesses to gain improvement, work where it's easiest to gain a result, harvest the low-hanging fruit, if you will, because the sense of progress will get you moving.

Moving is everything. When we feel stuck, it's easy to get locked into a pervasive, persistent and personal attitude. Once you start moving, you build momentum, and as you build momentum, things start to happen much more easily. You begin to feel more positive, a sense of progress, which, in turn, enables you to embrace more and so the cycle starts to lift you up.

It's important for you to be open to the towing support you receive from others and that you give it to others too, so there is an energy balance, but also that you let the support come and go. Use each little tug of support as a stepping stone to the next, and then the next, and so on. Letting go of attachment is helpful here, as it allows you to be in rhythm with the natural timing of things.

EXERCISE: NOTICE WHERE YOU ARE GETTING SUPPORT RIGHT NOW? APPRECIATE IT CONSCIOUSLY.

WHERE ELSE COULD YOU ASK FOR SUPPORT?

WHERE COULD YOU OFFER SUPPORT YOURSELF?
THAT WILL MAKE YOU FEEL BETTER TOO.

38. TAKE ACTION

Reading about something may make sense and initially put your mind at ease, as you will be able see the way forward. But this feeling is short-lived as we soon realize that nothing has changed. We read, take notes, and reflect on our own situation and gain a deeper understanding, and that helps with insight. But we only get a sense of knowing when we take action. A common trait is to want clarity before taking action, and I know it is one of my patterns of behaviour, but clarity arrives after taking action, that's when we get the real feedback, not just what our minds have imagined. So now you've done the inner work, and are clear about what you want, it's time to take action.

A quick Google search on the topic reminds me of the numerous – almost countless – things that are meant to help with taking action.

The important/urgent matrix is a key part of Steven Covey's work. The idea here is that the most valuable work we do is around the non-urgent important tasks, such as writing a book, developing the next product or programme and so on. However, we get sucked into the seemingly urgent and unimportant tasks such as email and social media. Being clear about your priorities allows you to focus on what's important.

Eat That Frog – the Brian Tracy classic, tells us to tackle our most unappealing, difficult task first, at the start of the day. This means the one you keep putting off, allowing the guilt and pressure to hang over your head and reduce your productivity throughout the day, affecting your sleep at night. Once you've tackled that task, you've not only pushed yourself into action, but you've released yourself from the negative burdens that went with it.

Timing – either set a five-minute timer to get you started on a project, on the basis that getting started is the hardest thing and once started you may actually carry on. Or you could adopt the Pomodoro technique, where you set the timer to 25-minute intervals and force yourself to work for that period, take a short break and repeat the process.

Then there's planning – "fail to plan, plan to fail" – which may mean writing down your important 'to-do' list the night before so that your subconscious works on it overnight and in the morning, you are clear what you are going to do.

There's accountability. If someone holds you to account (your boss, your spouse, your mastermind group, your coach), you are more likely to do the task as the fear of embarrassment when you show up not having delivered, spurs you into action.

The list is seemingly endless. And let's face it, it's all good stuff, it makes sense and it should work. However, in my experience, when I'm in the zone, in flow, or under last-minute time pressure, things get done. When I'm not, I could win national prizes for procrastination. I've even written notes on procrastination rather than deal with the matter in hand. The trick is to find a method that works for you.

EXERCISE: WHICH WAY OF GETTING THINGS DONE WORKS FOR YOU?

YOU'VE READ THE BOOK, YOU'VE DONE THE EXERCISES (YOU DID, DIDN'T YOU?), SO WHAT ARE YOU GOING TO DO DIFFERENTLY FROM NOW ON?

WHAT ARE THE MOST IMPORTANT BITS OF THIS BOOK FOR YOU? WHICH TOPICS RESONATED WITH YOU? WHY?

WHAT ARE YOU GOING TO DO WITH THESE INSIGHTS?

CHAPTER FOUR

THE CONCISE
ADVICE SERIES

The Success Book takes a high-level overview of the landscape of success, from personal mastery to creating triumphs and dealing with disasters. As success is personal to each and every one of us, this book suggests strategies to employ, offers insights and wisdom, and asks many questions designed to elicit deeper insight and thought from your good self.

Strategy is important, it's the overview, the broad plan or approach, its about the overall vision, it's about the meaning, the reason, the why – and that is what this book is about. However, for a strategy to become effective, it needs to be implemented, and that's where specific tactical skills become important. You need both strategy and tactics.

The following synopses of the other books in the LID Concise Advice Series will help you put your own success strategy into action.

THE FINANCIAL WELLBEING BOOK

One of the biggest enemies of our general wellbeing is stress; and one of the biggest causes of stress is concern about money. This book provides a simple and practical guide to planning your daily and long-term finances by understanding your objectives and motivations. In doing so, it offers respite from the anxiety and stress caused by money problems. The author, an experienced financial adviser, argues that the key to financial wellbeing is to "know thyself" in order to allow decisions to be made, and to ensure those decisions are the right ones for you. This is underpinned by having control of your daily finances, the ability to cope with a financial shock, having options in life, identifiable goals and a clear path to achieve them, and ensuring clarity and security for those we leave behind.

THE SMART THINKING BOOK

This book contains 60 pieces of distilled wisdom. Read each piece of advice in one minute, or the whole book in an hour. The sticky note format allows you to use the ideas for personal motivation, or to stimulate teams in meetings. Growth, communication, innovation, creativity, relationships and thinking are all covered. Inspire yourself and your business with some smart thinking.

THE PRODUCTIVITY HABITS

The pressure to be more productive is a nightmare for any business person – both at work and at home – but this doesn't have to be a problem anymore. This book introduces eight habits that can turn procrastination into productivity and the pain of overburden into the pleasure of achievement. As you read this book, you will develop productive habits allowing your 'to-do' list to dissolve effortlessly. The secret to unlocking each habit is explained in a compelling way and the book is packed with concise advice and engaging diagrams.

THE IMPACT CODE

The best leaders and managers create change. They are able to create a vision, communicate an idea and, in particular encourage action from others. What is it about these leaders and managers that makes others want to follow, engage and to act? The term "IMPACT" describes the effect we have on those around us. Having impact expresses the collective impression left by our visual appearance, our presence, the way we connect with others and the lasting effect we have on people when we have left the room. This book provides 50 short-but-powerful ways to raise your impact level in business. Taken together, it forms a code to enable you to create response in others and to ensure that every encounter (within your company and outside it) has the potential to bring something to you, whether financially, professionally or personally.

THE BRAIN BOOK

Our brain is our most valuable asset, and yet we are taught so little about it; the one thing that is involved in all your feelings, thoughts, and actions, and you're never given the manual. Consequently, few of us realize our potential. Recent developments in neuroscience demonstrate that your brain is like a muscle; you can increase your brainpower, and even change and develop your brain over time. Grounded in scientific research, this book gives you 50 ways to get more from your brain. You'll gain an understanding of how your brain works and how you can boost your mental performance. You'll discover how to improve your focus and memory, and how you can enhance your problem-solving skills. You'll even learn how you can programme your brain and keep it younger for longer.

THE DIAGRAMS BOOK

Many people find it difficult to express ideas and solve problems purely with words. They find it much easier to use diagrams. Distilled into this single, handy-sized volume are 50 of the best diagrams to help anyone with problem solving and thinking. Each of the 50 diagrams is presented on one spread, explained simply and accompanied by an exercise to help you apply them to your own situation. Now re-issued in a handy workbook format, The Diagrams Book is the ideal companion to The Ideas Book.

THE STORYTELLING BOOK

Business presentations could be simpler, more engaging and more effective, and our business lives could be much more rewarding if we were to restore the emotional power of storytelling. In an age that is data-rich but insight-poor, when people find themselves caught up in a system of numbers and spreadsheets, this book shows that the time has come to restore the lost art of storytelling; to put the 'author' back in 'authority'; to write less and think more. Through a step-by-step approach, the author shows that if we revert to our inherent role as storytellers we are more likely to be more effective and productive – and a lot less frustrated.

THE FUTURE BOOK

You have the ability to change it. If you know where to start. *The Future Book* is an inspirational manual for all of us who have an interest in making a change – in our lives, in our companies and in the world. Acclaimed futurologist Magnus Lindkvist has distilled his learning, stretching over two decades, to serve up an intense brew of inspirational insights, vivid examples and useful thinking tools. Drink this potion and open your eyes to the world of possibilities beyond the horizon, in the place we call 'future'.

THE FEEDBACK BOOK

Maintaining performance today is no longer simply about having an annual appraisal and telling employees "you must try harder". Research demonstrates that regular discussions about performance, and providing feedback to the people you manage, is a more effective way of motivating them and keeping them on track. Distilled into this single, handy-sized volume, are 50 tips, advice and techniques to help any manager to become skilled at discussing performance regularly, setting goals and objectives and providing the necessary feedback to ensure individuals and teams thrive in the company. Structured into five key sections, each of the 50 concise chapters also contains a practical exercise to help the reader understand and implement the concepts and ideas of this book.

THE NETWORKING BOOK

If you want to optimize your life – to exploit the full potential of your work life as well as your personal life – you need to connect with people. If you do not have a good and relevant network, you will have to contact a lot of people and beg them to help you. This could be humiliating! If you have an efficient network, a potential helper is already in your mind when you have a good idea or need assistance. There is no one way to be the perfect networker. Through discovering the authentic you, combined with the helpful tips in this book, you can create your personal unique way of networking.

THE MEETING BOOK

Across the world, businesses are searching for ways to work leaner and smarter. Working virtually across countries, time zones, and regions is, in theory, a good way to stay connected and keep travel and accommodation costs down. Businesses must be competent at working virtually in order to thrive, and meeting virtually is today's reality.

Technology companies are getting better and better at supporting meaningful virtual meetings and communication media is galloping ahead with people actively staying connected through social media and yet, at the same time, virtual business meetings are hitting a glass ceiling. This book suggests the human behaviour needed to make the most of these meetings is struggling to keep up. In this book, you will learn how to make meetings work for you, how to be present and how to be understood, why you suck at meetings today and what to do about it for tomorrow.

THE IDEAS BOOK

Coming up with ideas on your own can be hard. Doing it in brainstorms can be even harder. Following the success of *The Diagrams Book*, *The Ideas Book* explains 1) how to tackle tricky issues, 2) how to use inspirational techniques to generate smart ideas, and 3) how to get them underway. Each idea is shown on one spread, explained simply and accompanied by a short exercise to help you apply them to your situation.

THE MINDFULNESS BOOK

Research has told us that to be successful in our personal and professional lives, we need emotional intelligence; mindfulness is one practice to harness this ability and build your emotional capital. Mindfulness is an ancient Buddhist practice, which is very relevant for life today. Mindfulness is an integrative, mind/body-based approach that helps people to manage their thoughts and feelings by paying attention in a particular way: on purpose, in the present moment, and non-judgmentally. This increases awareness, clarity and acceptance of our present-moment reality.

This book reveals the seven dynamic emotions that create success, and provides a step-by-step guide to building emotional wealth and wellbeing.

CONCLUSION

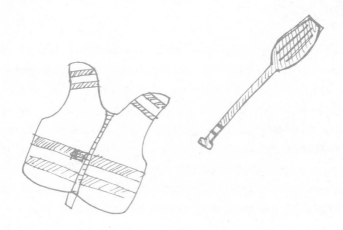

"MY TEACHING IS LIKE A RAFT USED TO CROSS THE RIVER.
ONLY A FOOL WOULD CARRY THE RAFT AROUND AFTER HE HAD
ALREADY REACHED THE OTHER SHORE OF LIBERATION"
(The Buddha)

So where do you go from here?

Success is personal to each and every one of us, but when you get
to know yourself and are able to live with yourself in silence without
distraction, when you get clear about what you want, and why, when you
learn to endure the inevitable setbacks with compassion and care for